maosm

'Maoism'

A Critique from the Left

Edited by Prasenjit Bose

Offset edition first published in May 2010.
Digital print edition, January 2020.

LeftWord Books
2254/2A Shadi Khampur
New Ranjit Nagar
New Delhi 110008
INDIA

www.leftword.com

LeftWord Books is a division of
Naya Rasta Publishers Pvt. Ltd.

ISBN 978-81-87496-61-8

Contents

Acknowledgements

This book is an outcome of a collective effort. Besides the contributors, the collection was made possible by Sudhanva Deshpande, Srinivasan Ramani and Albeena Shakil, who went through the manuscript at various stages, making incisive comments and valuable suggestions. The encouragement and guidance provided by Prakash Karat has also been a crucial input.

Dedicated to the victims of wanton violence . . .

Introduction

Prasenjit Bose

As the debate on leftwing extremist violence and the state's offensive against it intensifies in India, opinion tends to get increasingly polarized. On the one side are those who consider the CPI (Maoist) as a destructive terrorist group, much like the Islamist Lashkar-e-Taiba (LeT) or the separatist United Liberation Force of Asom (ULFA), which has to be crushed through the military might of the state. On the other side are those who see the Maoists as a revolutionary force, fighting for the cause of the exploited and the marginalized, and justify their violent acts as a necessary evil in order to bring about radical social transformation. Little effort is made, however, from either end to delve deeper into the question of leftwing extremism, in India or elsewhere, in order to understand its current activities in terms of its ideological basis, social roots and historical origins.

Many on the Right consider this to be an entirely fruitless exercise, because they see any effort to analyse the root causes of extremism and terrorism as an expression of empathy, which accords legitimacy to the extremist cause. Such a rightwing approach leads to foolhardiness, so vividly demonstrated by George Bush's 'war on terror'. That has not only led to unforgivable criminality in the form of imperialist invasions and occupations, killings and torture of innocents and destruction of entire societies; it has also singularly failed to combat extremism and terrorism. Rather, the extremist cause itself has received impetus across the world.

Some on the Left, however, go to the other extreme, especially when it comes to leftwing extremism. While very few come out explicitly espousing or defending the Maoist ideology, there is a tendency among others either to romanticize or to overlook their mindless violence and to one-sidedly berate the state for its security operations. This penchant for condoning acts of terror or glorifying violence in the name of radicalism – even that directed against innocent and helpless victims and not against the state –- is entirely opportunistic. Marx, writing in the context of the philosophical roots of religion, had said: 'To be radical is to grasp the root of the matter'.[1] Celebration of leftwing extremism and violence arises precisely out of the inability or the lack of willingness on the part of some thinkers, 'to grasp the root of the matter', and thereby terribly confuse form with content.

The present volume, which brings together three essays, looks at the question of left extremism from a Marxist standpoint. Left sectarianism, adventurism and dogmatism, as phenomena, are neither new nor unique to India. This collection of articles not only critiques its contemporary manifestation in India in the shape of the CPI (Maoist), but also traces its historical origins and record, both in the Indian context as well as internationally to show left sectarianism for what it is: a road to nowhere. But it is not simply an innocuous tendency, which surfaces within the Left from time to time. Historically, left sectarianism has been very counter-productive and it retains the potential of seriously damaging the prospects of the Left in future. The present volume therefore seeks to contribute to the ideological-political struggle against left sectarianism, by exposing its erroneous theoretical foundations and distorted praxis.

I

Lenin's 1920 work, *Leftwing Communism: An Infantile Disorder*, is a classic on the inner struggles and ideological debates within the international Communist movement in the early decades of the twentieth century. Lenin identified two tendencies which were inimical to the interests of the working class movement: 'opportunism', which 'developed into social-chauvinism and definitely sided with the bourgeoisie' and '*petty-bourgeois revolutionism,* which smacks of anarchism, or borrows something from the latter and, in all essential matters, does not measure up to the conditions and requirements of a consistently proletarian class struggle'.[2] On the latter tendency Lenin elaborated:

> A petty bourgeois driven to frenzy by the horrors of capitalism is a social phenomenon which, like anarchism, is characteristic of all capitalist countries. The instability of such revolutionism, its barrenness, and its tendency to turn rapidly into submission, apathy, phantasms, and even a frenzied infatuation with one

bourgeois fad or another – all this is common knowledge. However, a theoretical or abstract recognition of these truths does not at all rid revolutionary parties of old errors, which always crop up at unexpected occasions, in somewhat new forms, in a hitherto unfamiliar garb or surroundings, in an unusual – a more or less unusual – situation.

Anarchism was not infrequently a kind of penalty for the opportunist sins of the working class movement. The two monstrosities complemented each other.

Lenin's observations on 'leftwing communism' contain four crucial insights, which were not only accurate in the specific context in which they were made, but have continued to remain valid for the Communist movement. Firstly, left sectarianism is a reflection of a petty bourgeois class outlook, in contrast to a 'consistent proletarian' class outlook. Secondly, it is unstable, in the sense that it appears as a trend within the movement, peaks and then dissipates within a short span of time. Thirdly, despite being unstable, it does recur within the movement from time to time at certain conjunctures, since the social basis for such extremism always exist in capitalist societies. And fourthly, it often appears as a 'penalty for the opportunist sins' within the Left movement, and ideologically-politically 'complements' such opportunism.

Lenin's position vis-à-vis left sectarianism is enunciated by citing several concrete instances on which the Bolsheviks had to wage struggle against 'petty-bourgeois revolutionism', both within the party and outside (with the Socialist Revolutionary Party). For instance, left sectarianism had to be fought on the question of 'a strictly objective appraisal of the class forces and their alignment, before taking any political action'. This is vital for the Communist movement, because an overestimation of its own strength and underestimation of the strength of the enemy inevitably leads to adventurist actions and setbacks.

Then there was the question of violence and 'individual terrorism', which the left extremists considered to be the essential hallmark of revolutionism. Lenin states that this was something that 'we Marxists emphatically rejected', not because Marxists are opposed to violence 'in principle', but because it was not 'expedient' at all times. In essence, the context in which the Communists take to violence has to be very specific – Lenin cites the violence during the French revolution or that employed by 'a victorious revolutionary party which is besieged by the bourgeoisie of the whole world'. Being a revolutionary Marxist certainly does not imply being supportive of violence *per se*.

Lenin also underlined the struggle against the left sectarian tendency to 'sneer at the comparatively insignificant opportunist sins . . . while they themselves imitated the extreme opportunists . . .' This is precisely how the extreme left 'complements' opportunist tendencies within the Communist movement. Struggles against left deviation were conducted *within* the Bolshevik party too, most importantly, on the question of participation in 'a most reactionary parliament'. Lenin cites that the 'left' Bolsheviks had to be expelled from the party in 1908 for 'stubbornly refusing to understand the necessity of participating in a most reactionary parliament', at a time when the situation demanded that the party combined 'legal and illegal activities'.

It is noteworthy that the core issues in which the revolutionary movement in Russia witnessed intense ideological-political struggles between the Bolsheviks and the extreme left in the early decades of the twentieth century – on the correct assessment of the correlation of class forces at a given time, on violence and individual terrorism, on Communists' participation in bourgeois parliament, etc. – resurfaced time and again in different countries throughout the twentieth century, wherever the Communist movement was significant. Even today, these are precisely the issues, which mark the basic differences between the Communist and left sectarian trends.

II

The Communist movement in India was initiated in the backdrop of the freedom struggle in the 1920s. While the Communists did not succeed in acquiring the leadership of the national liberation movement against British colonialism, they played an important role by drawing in large sections of the working class and the peasantry within the ambit of the movement and influencing its overall direction. Following independence, alongside the emergence of the Communist party as a major opposition force to the ruling Congress party within the parliamentary democratic set up, ideological debates also intensified within the Left on the road to revolution in India. The initial debate surrounded the basic programmatic approach of the Communist movement, especially in regard to the characterization of the Indian state and the revolutionary strategy to be adopted.

On the one side of this debate were those who considered the independent Indian state as one, which was led by the national bourgeoisie, which was consistently anti-imperialist and had an anti-feudal character. From such a progres-sive characterization of 'Nehruvian socialism', it followed that the Communists would necessarily have to dovetail their revolutionary strategy to the efforts of the state led by the national bourgeoisie, which would eventually lead, through various transitory stages, to socialism. This class collaborationist and revisionist understanding was challenged by a significant section within the Communist party, which led to intense inner-party struggle during the 1950s and the eventual split in the Communist Party of India in 1964.

The Communist Party of India (Marxist) [CPI (M)], formed in 1964, arrived at a programmatic understanding that the Indian state is a bourgeois-landlord state led by the big bourgeoisie, which has a dual character. On the one hand the big bourgeoisie collaborates with imperialism in its pursuit of capitalist development. On the other hand, it has conflicts with imperialism in order to preserve and expand its economic domain, which it seeks to resolve through pressure, bargain and compromise. It is this dual character which gets manifested in the economic and foreign policies pursued by the Central Government. On the basis of such characterization of the Indian ruling classes and the state, a revolutionary strategy of building a peoples' democratic front – an alliance of workers, peasants and other toiling sections under working class leadership – was enunciated. The revolution, directed against the big bourgeoisie, landlordism and imperialism, is to be achieved by combining parliamentary and extra-parliamentary struggles. This overall understanding, however, was questioned by a small section, which considered participation in the parliamentary democratic process – just as the left sectarians did during Lenin's time – to be revisionist and non-revolutionary in principle.

Such left deviationist tendencies were always present within the Communist movement in India. It had surfaced vividly during the immediate aftermath of independence leading to errors like characterizing political independence as merely 'formal independence' and calling for armed insurrection against the newly independent state. These, however, were subsequently corrected and the Communists participated in the first general elections held in independent India in 1952. In the late 1960s, however, left sectarianism reappeared on the scene. This was the period when land struggles under Communist leadership were gaining momentum in West Bengal, drawing in large sections of the peasantry. The Congress was losing ground, and after the 1967 state assembly elections the first non-Congress United Front Government was formed in West Bengal, in which the CPI (M) participated. The same year, extreme left elements who were opposing the participation of the CPI (M) in elections, led a violent peasant revolt in Naxalbari in the Darjeeling district of north Bengal, and gave a call for armed insurrection to overthrow the state.

Significantly, the Chinese Communist Party (CPC), which had itself come under the grip of left sectarianism during this period – culminating in the 'cultural revolution' – openly backed the left adventurists in India. *People's Daily*, the official organ of the CPC, published an editorial on July 5, 1967, entitled 'Spring Thunder Breaks Over India', where it hailed the Naxalbari revolt because 'armed struggle is the only correct road for the Indian revolution . . . the spark in Darjeeling will start a prairie fire . . .'. Encouraged by such prognoses and prescriptions, naxalites in India borrowed wholesale from the strategy of the Chinese revolution developed in the 1930s and 1940s along with the CPC's concepts and formulations of the Indian state and society put forward in the late 1960s. They went to great lengths to portray themselves as the flag bearers of the 'Chinese line', even coining the slogan: 'China's chairman is our chairman, Chinese path is our path'. When the CPI (ML) was formed in 1970, its programme stated:

> The democratic revolution in India is taking place in the era of Mao Tse-tung when world imperialism is heading for total collapse and socialism is advancing towards worldwide victory. *Our revolution is a part of the great proletarian cultural revolution* which has consolidated socialism and proletarian dictatorship in China and has turned China into the reliable base area of world revolution. Our revolution is taking place at a time…when the CPC headed by Chairman Mao and Vice-Chairman Lin Piao is leading the international proletariat to fulfill its historic mission

of emancipating the whole of mankind from the rule of imperialism and reaction and establishing socialism and communism on this earth. *We are a contingent of this great army of the international proletariat.* (Emphasis added.)

Thus, from their very inception, left sectarians in India have believed in a one size fits all theory of revolution – that of imitating the Chinese path. They never felt the need to seriously engage with Indian society, understand its socio-economic realities and its historical and cultural specificities. They trashed the experience of the Indian Communist movement during the freedom struggle as well as the post-independence period. Most importantly, they misestimated the correlation of class forces and misread the mood among the masses. Their dogma was simple: the situation is always ripe for a revolution, and if revolution succeeded in China by following a certain path, the only thing that needed to be done was to emulate it in India at all costs.

The naxalite folly, in relying upon such imported know-how to make revolution and trying to blindly imitate it, became amply clear within a very short span. The armed rebellions led by the left adventurists in some rural pockets of West Bengal and Andhra Pradesh were either crushed by the state or fizzled out by 1970–71. Not only did their unrealistic slogans fail to arouse the peasantry, their mindless violence and individual terrorism alienated the masses. The attempts to spread anarchy in the urban areas in the name of 'cultural revolution' further isolated them and invited more state repression. By the time of their leader Charu Mazumdar's death in police custody in 1972, the 'spring thunder' had ended in a whimper.

The CPC had realised by 1970 that the naxalite movement in India was going nowhere and was turning into an embarrassment. It is reported that the CPC sent a note to Charu Mazumdar expressing its reservations over the activities of the CPI (ML) some time in 1970–71.[3] The main criticisms made by the CPC were directed against the description of Mao Zedong as India's chairman, secret assassinations, making bloodletting the yardstick for the revolutionary fervour of a member, ignoring mass work and mass struggle, confusing military tactics with political and organizational issues, and misrepresenting united front tactics. However, the damage had already been done.

III

The failure of the naxalite movement in India in the 1970s did lead to some reflection on the part of those who had been its active participants, but the weakness of their theoretical foundations and concepts came in the way of any meaningful introspection and course correction. Significant changes took place within the CPC itself in the 1970s, especially after the death of Mao Zedong, and the errors of the cultural revolution were finally put to rest in 1978. So dependent and fragile was the ideological framework of the CPI (ML) that it could not come to grips with those changes, eventually leading to innumerable splits in the 1970s and 1980s.[4]

In practice, the main debate within the naxalites has always been on whether their activities would remain to be based on individual annihilation of 'class enemies' or to reorient their work prioritizing mass activities and participating in the democratic process. Some naxalite groups, like the CPI (ML) Liberation and the CPI (ML) New Democracy, eventually abandoned armed struggle and joined the parliamentary democratic process. However, other groups like the CPI (ML) Peoples' War and the Maoist Communist Centre continued with their violent tactics and eventually merged in 2004 to form the CPI (Maoist). The programme of the CPI (Maoist), which is at the forefront of leftwing extremism in India today, envisages as its central task, the 'seizure of political power by armed struggle'; a throwback to the same old Chinese path.

The experience of the Communist movement in India has already shown the futility of a blind pursuit of armed struggle against the Indian state. In a context where parliamentary democracy has taken root, resort to armed struggle without exhausting the potential for mass mobilization within the democratic set up, not only fails in its objective but also turns the masses away. Moreover, the socio-economic realities today, in India and abroad, are very different from the situation in the 1960s and 1970s, when socialism existed as a major countervailing force to imperialism. We are currently in an era where international finance-driven imperialism dominates economically, militarily and culturally, posing stiffer challenges before the Communist movement.

Left politics itself has undergone a sea change globally, especially since the fall of the Soviet Union, with newer questions of democracy, peoples' participation and social justice acquiring added significance. The need has been felt within the Left, especially among Communists across the globe, to renew and enrich the vision for socialism in keeping with the momentous changes that have taken place over the past two decades. Some parties with a left extremist past have also seriously engaged with these questions, most notably the Nepalese Maoists, and have repositioned themselves within the democratic process. For the contemporary left sectarians in India, however, the answer to all such questions is to be found in guerilla warfare and 'liberated zones'.

The current activities of the CPI (Maoist), across their pockets of existence in the remote forest areas in India's central-eastern region, bear out the degeneration that inevitably follows from dogmatism. The typical tactics of the Maoists have been to build their base areas in the jungles near tribal habitats and establish their control over the area through the force of the gun, eliminating or terrorizing all other political parties and tribal organizations into submission. The Maoists do not believe in organizing the tribals for exercising their rights over land and forest resources or for socio-economic development.[5] Their sole aim is to set up the so-called 'liberated zones', where the entry of all other state or non-state actors is prohibited by force and no political activities other than their own are permissible. These 'liberated zones' are then used to launch armed attacks in other areas against the state machinery, not only the police stations and paramilitary outposts but often targeting railway tracks, roads, power stations, telecom facilities and even schools and health centres. Political opponents are often executed after conducting kangaroo courts and labeling them 'police informers'. Extortion from forest contractors and the mining mafia is the primary means of financing these activities.[6] Such nihilist anarchism perpetrated in the name of 'people's war', and the eventual retaliation by the state, brings immense suffering to the tribals and other forest dwelling communities, shattering their lives and livelihoods.

Even as the Maoists issue calls for boycott of elections, they forge underhand deals with individual leaders and candidates of bourgeois political parties during elections and indulge in booth capturing in their favour in exchange for money, protection and patronage. This has happened repeatedly in Bihar, Jharkhand, Orissa and more recently in West Bengal. They also assassinate elected representatives from different political parties at the behest of their rivals. For instance, the Jharkhand

Mukti Morcha (JMM) MP Sunil Mahato was killed in Ghatshila by the Maoists in March 2007. They also made assassination attempts against the former Andhra Pradesh Chief Minister in 2003 and the West Bengal Chief Minister in November 2008.

It is noteworthy that the cadres of Left formations, especially the CPI (M) – mostly belonging to the toiling classes and socially deprived sections – are specifically targeted by the CPI (Maoist) and assassinated on a frequent basis. They see the presence of a significant Left force in India's political mainstream and their success as a big impediment in furthering their left extremist agenda. While the Left as a whole has to traverse a long way to eventually succeed in its revolutionary objective in India, it has over the years played a consistent and significant role in defending people's rights and deepening democracy. In the past two decades the Left emerged as the ideological-political core around which the resistance and struggles against communalism, neoliberal policies and imperialism have been built. The Left-led state governments, despite their limited powers, have successfully implemented pro-people policies like land redistribution and democratic decentralization, which have benefited the peasantry and the working people and expanded the mass appeal of the Left. All this is anathema to the left sectarians.

Much of their current violence is therefore directed against the Left, especially in the CPI (M) stronghold of West Bengal. No political party anywhere in India has lost as many activists and supporters to Maoist terror, as has the CPI (M) in West Bengal since 2008. What is worse, this mayhem is being conducted in league with the main rightwing opposition to the Left Front in West Bengal, the Trinamul Congress, with the avowed aim of bringing them into power in the state in the 2011 assembly elections. This gang-up with right reactionary forces in order to settle scores with the Communist Left marks the climax of degeneration for the Maoists in India.

IV

The present volume seeks to make an intervention in this backdrop. All the three essays contained in this volume deal with left sectarianism, with two focusing on the CPI (Maoist) in India and one with the international experience of left adventurism. The first essay by P.M.S. Grewal is a theoretical critique of the programmatic understanding of the Indian Maoists. Grewal revisits the earlier debates within the Indian Communist movement, tracing the origins of left sectarianism, to show how the Maoists of today have remained prisoners of the old dogmas regarding the Indian state and society as well as the revolutionary path. He exposes the theoretical hollowness of the Maoists and blows up the myth about their being a revolutionary force fighting for the cause of the tribals or other exploited sections. The last section of the essay provides detailed information on the recent Maoist attacks against the CPI (M) and the Left in Lalgarh and elsewhere.

Nilotpal Basu's essay complements Grewal's analysis, by looking at the flawed ideological political approach of the Maoists, which negates the very first principles of Marxism-Leninism. Basu argues that the greatness of Mao Zedong lies precisely in his creative application of Marxism in the concrete conditions of Chinese society in the 1930s and 1940s and not in mechanically implementing the Comintern line on how to carry out the revolution in China. In contrast, the Indian Maoists seek to re-enact the Chinese revolution in contemporary Indian conditions, which are vastly different from those in pre-revolutionary China. The farcical end result is the very anti-thesis of Mao Zedong thought. Basu makes a robust critique of the anti-democratic practices of the Maoists and their hypocritical sympathizers. He also argues that Maoists can be effectively dealt with, not by means of imposing bans or security measures alone, but by ensuring their political isolation and addressing the developmental needs of the tribal areas where the Maoists operate.

Vijay Prashad looks at the international experience of left extremism, especially in Latin America. Through very informative expositions of the major political developments within the Left in countries like Venezuela, Brazil, Cuba, Peru and Colombia, Prashad argues that the present day realities do not favour guerilla warfare any more. Prashad contrasts the failure of armed struggles in country after country with the successful 'long march through the institutions' by the Latin American Left, and draws the conclusion that the way forward for the Left lies in mass movements and not guns. The discussion on the Maoists in Peru and Philippines is particularly relevant in the Indian context as it demonstrates similar tendencies within the extreme left leading to very similar and equally destructive outcomes.

We also reproduce as an annexure, excerpts from a CPI (M)

document, *Ideological Debate Summed Up*, which was first published in June 1968. This document throws light on the ideological debates within the Communist movement in India in the 1960s. The relevant excerpts from the document reproduced here deal with all the ideological questions thrown up by the naxalites – whether India's independence was merely 'formal', whether the Indian big bourgeoisie was 'comprador', whether the state was 'neocolonial' and a 'puppet' of imperialism, whether to take part in the parliamentary democratic process and participate in coalition governments in the states. This document serves as an appropriate historical backgrounder to the Marxist critique of contemporary left sectarianism in India. It contains an important and enduring vision – that the road to revolution in India will neither be the Chinese road nor the Russian road, but a distinct Indian road.

NOTES

[1] Karl Marx, Introduction to *A Contribution to the Critique of Hegel's Philosophy of Right*, 1844.

[2] The discussion here is based on the chapter 'The Struggle Against Which Enemies Within the Working-Class Movement Helped Bolshevism Develop, Gain Strength, and Become Steeled'.

[3] See Biplab Dasgupta, *The Naxalite Movement*, Allied Publishers, 1974. In Chapter 7 (p. 195) Dasgupta refers to an inner-party note submitted by Ashim Chatterjee titled 'Bartaman Partyr Kajer Sar Sankalan' (in Bengali) where he accuses Charu Mazumdar of suppressing the CPC note because it contained criticism of his policies. Later the main points in the Chinese note were circulated among the members of the CPI (ML) in a letter signed among others by Kanu Sanyal and C. Tejeswar Rao.

[4] For a detailed discussion on the ideological-political basis of the splintering of the naxalites in the 1970s and 1980s, see Prakash Karat, 'Naxalism Today: At an Ideological Deadend', *The Marxist*, Jan-March, 1985.

[5] For instance, the Maoists have remained conspicuously absent in the struggles to defend the forest rights of the tribals waged by various democratic organisations alongside the Communists, which eventually led to the enactment of the Tribal Forest Rights Act in the Indian parliament in 2006. Moreover, unlike the late 1960s when the naxalites attempted to organize tribal peasant revolts, the contemporary Maoists take absolutely no interest in organizing the peasantry, either against landlords or the state's anti-peasant policies.

[6] See for instance Arundhati Roy's article 'Walking with the Comrades', *Outlook*, March 29, 2010. While glorifying the Maoists and supporting their armed struggle in Chhattisgarh, she also provides an account of Maoist extortion. She states that the forest contractors who buy *tendu* leaves from the tribals pay Rs. 120 per bag as 'commission' to the 'party'. This source alone provides hundreds of crores to the Maoists. For an effective critique of Roy's position, see Sudhanva Deshpande's rejoinder 'She was There', *Outlook*, April 12, 2010.

Indian Maoists
Flawed Strategy and Perverted Praxis

P.M.S. Grewal

The Communist Party of India (Maoist) came into existence in 2004 through the merger of the Maoist Communist Centre of India (MCC) and the CPI (ML) People's War Group. It has come into the limelight through reckless acts of violence in Chhattisgarh, Jharkhand, Orissa, West Bengal and Maharashtra – not through any meaningful achievement won for the tribals or peasants whose cause they claim to uphold. The gruesome massacre of 11 tribal villagers in the Jamui district of Bihar, brutal assassinations of student activists, poor tribal peasants and school teachers in West Medinipur district of West Bengal and the abduction and beheading of a police sub-inspector in Jharkhand in the recent past starkly illustrate the mindless nature of the so-called 'People's War' that the Maoists claim to be waging against the Indian state. The organized Left, especially the CPI (M), is being specifically targeted by the Maoists. Of the over 190 members and supporters of the CPI (M) killed by anti-Left forces in West Bengal since 2009, more than half have been murdered in cold blood by the Maoists.

Many in the bourgeois media, while highlighting such heinous activities, have sought to accord a romantic halo to the Maoists. Sections of it have gone to the extent of painting the Maoists as the real Left which fights for the oppressed as against the organized Left often dubbed as the 'official' or 'parliamentary' Left. The UPA Government has done its bit to project the Maoists by playing a cynical game. This consists of, on the one hand calling them the gravest threat to internal security and on the other turning a blind eye to the support rendered to them by its own constituent the Trinamul Congress. Needless to say, all this has aided the Maoist cause. The Maoist challenge cannot be met by mere administrative measures without politically isolating them among the masses. For this it is necessary to expose the left sectarian, adventurist and anarchist nature of their ideology, strategy and tactics.

LEFT SECTARIANISM: THE BACKGROUND

Left sectarianism is not new to the Indian Communist movement. It had surfaced in the CPI during 1948–51. Its main features were: characterizing Indian independence as formal, dubbing the Indian ruling class as the stooge of British imperialism and call for a forcible seizure of power on the presumption of the existence of a revolutionary situation. The failure of this line in practice forced the CPI to abandon it.

Later this trend re-emerged in 1967–68 under the label of naxalism, three years after the split in the CPI and formation of the CPI (M) in 1964. The founding Party Congress of the CPI (M), in which the party adopted its programme, had deferred discussion on ideological issues. Immediately after the Congress, most of its top leadership was imprisoned and the task of debating and clinching ideological issues could not be carried forward. At the same time the Communist Party of China (CPC), which had initially taken correct positions vis-à-vis revisionism of the Communist Party of Soviet Union (CPSU), moved to a left sectarian position and began characterizing India as a neo-colony and the Indian Government a client of imperialism. The prestige of the CPC and its overt support to the naxalites aided the emergence of this left sectarian trend and the formation of the CPI (ML) in 1970.

The naxalites believed that India is not politically independent but semi-colonial and semi-feudal; that the Indian state is controlled by imperialists, comprador bureaucratic capital and feudal landlords; and the stage of revolution is national liberation against imperialism, comprador capitalism and feudalism. From this it followed that people's war based on armed struggle of the peasantry is the only possible tactical line for liberation. The naxalites also characterized the Soviet Union as revisionist (later modified to 'social imperialist') and alleged that it was collaborating with US imperialism. They condemned participation in parliament as reformist and adopted poll boycott as a strategic slogan; they denied the role of mass organizations and abandoned trade unions as reformist organizations. Further in the sphere of tactics, they negated the role of united fronts, branding them as class collaborationist. This understanding was accompanied by an assessment that the conditions were ripe for revolution and that all it required was for groups of determined individuals to launch armed actions and the people would rise in revolt and overthrow the ruling classes. This gross overestimation of the situation was vividly captured in the naxalite slogan: 'a single spark will light the prairie fire'.

Naxalite activity in the countryside during 1969–71 consisted of armed struggle based on annihilation of individuals that led to the elimination of few *jotedars* and petty officials. The naxalites displayed utter disdain towards organizing struggles of the peasantry on their partial demands on the grounds that this would act as a dampener on the 'revolutionary fervour' of the peasantry and endanger the cause of the impending revolution. This contempt towards developing the revolutionary mass movement was symptomatic of looking for short cuts to revolution so characteristic of petty bourgeois radicalism the world over. Their slogan of armed struggle did not find many takers among the peasantry. Even in areas where they managed to attract sections of tribal peasants, the non-tribal peasants remained aloof. It is this inability to rally the peasantry, and the state repression that followed acts of individual annihilation, that led to the failure of their so-called uprisings in Naxalbari, Gopiballabhpur, Srikakulam, and elsewhere. Meanwhile the peasantry in West Bengal increasingly rallied behind the land struggles led by the Krishak Sabha and the CPI (M).

Following this failure, the naxalites, especially in West Bengal shifted their arena of operations to Calcutta and other urban centres. Here too they were unable to attract the working class and relied primarily on students and other petty bourgeois sections as well as lumpen elements. The 'elimination of class enemies' in urban areas took the form of assassinating traffic policemen, other minor officials and even the vice-chancellor of a university. Their real fire was, however, directed at the CPI (M), which was perceived as the main hurdle in the way of their march to revolution. Murderous attacks were unleashed against CPI (M) leaders and cadres, often along with Congress goons, during the period of semi-fascist terror in the state perpetrated by the Indira Gandhi-led Congress. This earned them the ignominy of being called *Congshals*.[1] They were unable to sustain these tactics and by mid-1972 their 'urban uprising' had virtually fizzled out.

The failure of the naxalite line of individual annihilation to attract the rural or urban masses, their inability to set up a disciplined Party and reliance on spontaneity of action squads over which the Party had little or no control led to serious differences that ultimately led to their disintegration. The first split in the CPI (ML) took place in 1971, i.e., within one year of its foundation. The debates and inner-Party struggle within the CPC also influenced this process. Since then the naxalites splintered into innumerable groups. Of these groups, the PWG over time came to acquire a limited base in remote tribal areas of Andhra Pradesh and Chhattisgarh. Another left sectarian group, the MCC – which was not originally part of the CPI (ML) – also became active in areas of Bihar and present-day Jharkhand. The PWG was later decimated in Andhra Pradesh and were unable to build any significant base among the non-tribal peasantry in any part of the country. Given their ideological construct, organizing the urban working class never really featured on their agenda. The CPI (Maoist), which today represents the leading naxalite formation in India, was formed with the coming together of the CPI (ML) PW and the MCC in 2004.

FLAWED PROGRAMME

The CPI (Maoist) virtually remains a prisoner to the left sectarian formulations of the CPI (ML) Programme of 1970. It also refuses to draw any lessons from the failure of the naxalite movement and chooses to remain blind to the momentous changes that have taken place in India and the world during the last forty years. Like petty bourgeois anarchists the world over, its theory and practice reveals a skewed understanding of the international and national correlation of class forces, shrill rhetoric and adventurist actions that render stellar service to the very ruling classes it claims to fight.

Hollow Understanding of Contemporary Imperialism

The CPI (Maoist) Programme claims to draw its ideological inspiration from Marxism-Leninism-Mao Zedong Thought. The programme of a Communist Party in essence outlines the strategy of revolution in the particular country in which it works. Such a strategy is based on a concrete analysis of the economy, politics and society of that country. However, no correct strategy for revolution in any country can be arrived upon without an accurate analysis of the correlation of class forces on the international arena. This must incorporate as its integral part a concrete analysis of contemporary imperialism and arrive at an objective assessment of the strengths and weaknesses of the forces of socialism on a world scale. It is precisely here that the hollowness of the Maoist ideological construct is most starkly revealed.

Their Programme confines itself to a generalized mention of the role of imperialism vis-à-vis India and has very little to say about the operations of imperialism on a world scale. Most strikingly, there is no analysis of imperialist globalization, which has reshaped the contours of world capitalism since the late 1970s. The unprecedented concentration and internationalization of finance capital, its speculative nature, global mobility and role in assaulting the sovereignty of nations in its quest to get unimpeded access to their economies have no significance for the Maoists' Programme. The accompanying intensification of exploitation of the working class and other toilers and the increasing concentration of wealth and assets in the hands of the MNCs and the international financial conglomerates too does not merit their attention. Neither is there any mention of the shifts in the accumulation regime and the role of the state under neoliberal capitalism, savage cuts in wages and welfare benefits for the workers, restructuring of the capitalist production process, jobless growth and increasing casualization and informalization of labour. They also fail to see the nature of technological progress and growth of productive forces achieved under advanced capitalism and the utilization of this by imperialist ruling classes to overcome, however temporarily, the crisis tendencies inherent within capitalism.

Similarly, there is no proper analysis of US militarism, the most visible face of imperialism today. Imperialist aggression and wars aimed at suppressing national liberation struggles or 'rolling back Communism' in the latter half of the twentieth century are all perfunctorily dismissed as 'proxy wars' waged between imperialism and the erstwhile Soviet Union. Moreover, for a Programme adopted in 2004, it is shocking that there is not even a mention of the 'war on terror' unleashed by the US, its invasions and occupations in Afghanistan or Iraq and the imperialist machinations in the Middle East or Latin America. This shows that even as they claim imperialism to be one of the three main enemies or targets of the Indian revolution, the Maoists feel no need to comprehend this enemy in its totality. Little wonder that their anti-imperialism remains a mere slogan. It does not manifest in mass mobilization and visibly demonstrated opposition to either the doings of imperialism on a world scale or even the concrete manifestations of imperialist penetration within India.

Denial of Socialism

The naxalites of the late 1960s and early 1970s had concluded that capitalism had been restored in the Soviet Union and that the latter had transmuted into 'social imperialism', which was then dubbed the greatest enemy of the people of the world, greater even than US imperialism. True to this tradition, the Maoists' Programme states that capitalism was restored in Soviet Union in 1956 after the demise of Stalin and 'it further emerged as a social imperialist and thereby a super power by 1970' which 'started to exploit many oppressed countries and nations . . . emerged as a great danger and vicious enemy of the world people . . . emerged as the chief rival of US imperialism for redivision and hegemony' leading to loss of several million lives 'in several proxy wars'.

This amounts to standing history on its head. For all its shortcomings and mistakes, only the motivated can deny the role of the Soviet Union in helping maintain world peace for several decades after the Second World War and curbing to an extent, the aggressive designs of US imperialism. The Maoists also wish away the positive role played by the Soviet Union in supporting national liberation struggles in South East Asia, Latin America and Africa and buys into the US imperialist propaganda, that it was responsible for the loss of millions of lives. It fails to objectively assess the role of aid provided by the Soviet Union to different Third World countries in helping them to both pursue a relatively independent path of development and to resist imperialist pressures in some measure. The setbacks to socialism following the collapse of the Soviet Union, its impact on changing the world correlation of forces in favour of imperialism and the consequent tendency of the ruling classes of developing countries to succumb and collaborate with imperialism are a damning indictment of the Maoists' thesis about the role of Soviet Union.

By the same yardstick, the Maoists' Programme states that China became capitalist after the death of Mao Zedong in 1976. It provides no explanations or analysis regarding its formulations about restoration of capitalism in Soviet Union and China. There is neither any analysis of what went wrong in the course of building socialism nor any explanation of how the trajectories and outcomes in Russia and China have differed markedly since the 1980s. In their blinkered worldview, there is no socialist country in the world today. Not even Cuba is mentioned. Nor do they have anything to say about the growth of anti-imperialist movements in Latin America leading to the installation of progressive anti-imperialist regimes in Venezuela, Bolivia and other countries. That the Programme of a party which claims to be part of the world revolutionary struggle for socialism has nothing to learn from the experiences of building socialism in the twentieth century, nor any inspiration to draw from the existing socialist regimes, speaks volumes of its commitment to socialism.

While the international correlation of forces continues to favour imperialism today, the fact remains that capitalism is a crisis-ridden system of exploitation, oppression and injustice, which has once again been exposed through the recent experience of the global economic crisis. The only system which can provide an alternative to capitalism, remains socialism and therefore the central social contradiction for this epoch remains that between imperialism and socialism. In failing to either appreciate the positive experiences of socialism in the last century or learn from its shortcomings and mistakes, the Maoists are basically in a denial mode which only serves to undermine the socialist cause.

Warped View of Anti-Imperialist Movements

The naxalites of the 1970s and 1980s were very vocal in asserting that national liberation struggles are the sole motor force of world revolution. This view came from the CPC's Three Worlds Theory. This theory placed the two 'superpowers' – Soviet Union and USA – in the First World, countries allied to the 'superpowers' in the Second World, and the entire Asia (except Japan), Africa and Latin America in the Third World. The CPC advocated that world revolution would be achieved through the countryside, i.e. the Third World encircling the First and Second Worlds. However, the practice of the naxalites did not match their assertions. Drawing inspiration from the left sectarian understanding of the CPC during the cultural revolution, they opposed several national liberation struggles, especially in Africa as in the case of Angola and Mozambique, which were supported by the Soviet Union.

The present-day Maoists too acclaim national liberation as the mainstay of world revolution. Their document *Strategy and Tactics of the Indian Revolution* states: 'The countries of Asia, Africa and Latin America are the storm centres of world revolution dealing deadly blows against imperialism'. However, they do not mention even one country in that document where those 'deadly blows' to imperialism are being dealt by revolutionaries. The only forces in the third world that seem to have inspired the Maoists are the *jehadists* and LTTE. A statement issued by their Politbureau after the 15th Lok Sabha Elections makes a positive assessment of the upsurge in the activities of *jehadist* forces in Pakistan in the following words: 'In South Asia, the second focal point of national liberation struggles in the contemporary world, the situation has continued to be explosive with militant uprisings in several parts of Pakistan such as the Swat Valley, North West Provinces, FATA, and other regions.'[2] That they consider the *jehadist* reactionaries to be anti-imperialists fighting for national liberation is also made clear by the CPI (Maoist) Politbureau member, Koteshwar Rao alias Kishanji in his interview to *Hindustan Times* of June 9, 2009, where he states that, 'We feel the Islamic upsurge should not be opposed as it is basically anti-US and anti-imperialist in nature. We therefore want it to grow.'

This entirely opportunistic stand has been succinctly exposed for what it is by a well-known naxalite sympathizer in the following words:

> . . . the Islamic jihadist forces (Taliban, Al Qaida, Lashkar-e-Toiba and other militant outfits operating in the sub-continent) had repeatedly made it clear that their goal is the setting up of an Islamic state based on strict religious shariat laws, which ban democratic political activities, curtail women's free movement, impose orthodox feudal practices and customs, etc. . . . [T]he CPI (Maoist) is supporting these Islamic religious fundamentalist jihadists, just because they are opposing the US. So, any stick is good enough to beat the US? The party fails to analyse their class character and opportunist politics, and forgets that the Taliban, Al Qaida, etc., which lead the 'Islamic upsurge' today, were created by the US CIA to overthrow the pro-Soviet regime in Afghanistan.[3]

The statement of the CPI (Maoist) Politbureau referred to above also rues the decimation of the LTTE in Sri Lanka as having 'a negative effect on the revolutionary movement in India as well as South Asia and the world at large.' Here again, a semi-fascist formation that excelled in the assassination of all political rivals and whose adventurist strategy to achieve a separate *Tamil Eelam* led to the deaths of lakhs of Tamils, which had never displayed even a pretence of anti-imperialism, is passed off as a revolutionary organization fighting for national liberation. This thoroughly exposes the hollowness of the Maoists' programmatic understanding itself which leads to such warped understanding about anti-imperialist movements and national liberation struggles.

Erroneous Characterization of Indian State and Society

In their *Strategy and Tactics of the Indian Revolution*, the Maoists characterize the Indian state as being, 'semi-colonial and semi-feudal under neo-colonial form of indirect rule, exploitation and control.' They seek to justify their thesis about India being a semi-colony in the following words:

> After the British colonialists were compelled to give up their direct rule . . . power was transferred to their compradors – the big bourgeoisie and the big landlords . . . Several imperialist powers took the place of British imperialism in oppressing and exploiting our country. It is these imperialist powers that actually control the politics, economy and culture and decide almost all the vital policies of the ruling classes of India under the sign board of formal independence that is fake in essence.

This is almost a facsimile of the analysis of Chinese society made by Mao Zedong in his work *The Chinese Revolution and the Chinese Communist Party* in 1939. When Mao characterized pre-revolutionary Chinese society as semi-colonial he was talking about a country divided into spheres of influence by different imperialist powers, including a significant part over which the Japanese imperialists exercised direct military control. There was no central government worth its name. Besides imperialist depredations, the people were also subject to the oppressive rule of different warlords engaged in internecine warfare. Capitalism had just begun to develop, the national bourgeoisie was weak, and comprador sections linked with different imperialist powers exercised far bigger influence. The comprador big bourgeoisie in China derived their sustenance from the imperialist powers and worked to perpetuate China's semi-colonial status.

It is sheer ignorance about Chinese as well as Indian history which leads the Maoists to find 'basic similarities in the conditions between India and pre-revolutionary China'. Unlike China, India was a direct colony under British rule. Even under the colonial rule, significant sections of the Indian bourgeoisie had developed an industrial base and were supportive of the national liberation movement led by the Congress. The defeat of fascism in the Second World War and the emergence of the socialist bloc under the leadership of the Soviet Union had changed the correlation of forces on a world scale. These developments weakened imperialism and provided a tremendous boost to national liberation struggles the world over. Within India, there was a huge anti-imperialist and anti-feudal upsurge after the Second World War, where the Communists also played a major role. That forced the British imperialists to strike a compromise with the Congress and the Muslim League and quit India in 1947. Through the establishment of Congress rule in independent India, it was the big bourgeoisie – along with the landlords – which had acquired state power.

If the Maoists are to be believed, however, the only change brought about by independence was that the direct rule of the British imperialists was replaced by the indirect rule of different imperialist powers immediately after 1947. *Strategy and Tactics of the Indian Revolution* states: 'after the so-called independence, the imperialist exploitation of the Indian people has not only remained uninterrupted but has also tremendously increased'. They never care to explain how a weakened imperialism could possibly exercise such control within less than half a decade of the end of the Second World War? Even the CPC did not consider India to be a semi-colony of different imperialist powers till 1959–60, when Indo-China border tensions heightened. At the root of the Maoist folly lies their flawed assessment of the character and role of the bourgeoisie in third world countries like India and their refusal to take note of the development of capitalism in these countries. To this we shall return later.

The other major Maoists formulation about the character of Indian society is that of its being 'semi-feudal'. This amounts to grossly underplaying the growth of capitalist relations in agriculture since independence. Nobody would deny that there are some regions in the country where old forms of landlordism continue to exist and, in the absence of thoroughgoing land reforms in most states, land continues to be monopolised in the hands of the few. However, the major trend in agrarian relations has been the development of capitalist relations in the countryside, characterized by the proletarianization of large sections of the rural working masses. This is reflected in the huge number of agricultural workers as a proportion of the rural population.[4] Since independence, rural India also witnessed the accelerated differentiation of the peasantry and the large-scale eviction of tenants holding traditional leases. The increased levels of re-investment of capital in agriculture and agriculture-related activity by the rural rich, particularly landlords, alongwith production for the market, laid the basis for the development of capitalism in Indian agriculture. This process was supported by the policies of the state, which provided support, protection and subsidies to agriculture, thereby consolidating the position of the landlords and rich peasants. State sponsored development of agriculture (green revolution) and acquiring self sufficiency in foodgrains production would not have been possible in India, had it been a semi-feudal society.

In the post-liberalization period, state support has been gradually withdrawn and the peasantry has been exposed to global markets dominated by agribusiness corporations. This has precipitated an agrarian crisis of acute proportions, affecting all sections of the peasantry. While landlordism remains the fundamental barrier to progressive agrarian change in third world societies like India, the imperialist penetration in agriculture now poses an added challenge. The solution to the agrarian question today therefore involves both direct class struggle against landlordism, moneylender-merchant exploitation and caste and gender oppression in the countryside, as well as the struggle against the new onslaught on agriculture by imperialism and the domestic bourgeoisie. The agricultural policies of the state have become an important site of class struggle in this context.

The Maoists, however, remain clueless about the agrarian situation in India. Their Programme contains starkly contradictory formulations, as exemplified in Para 15:

> Leaving aside a handful of big landlords, including some newly emerged big pro-capitalist landlords (from among the old rich peasants), the vast majority of the peasantry, particularly the poor peasants and agricultural labourers, as well as a sizable section of the middle peasants, continue to be increasingly driven into the

clutches of the usurers, merchants, big pro-capitalist landlords, whereas the grip of the Banks and other financial institutions also continues to tighten further and further. With the increasing penetration of imperialist finance capital, its grip has been further tightened. This has also further introduced some capitalist relations of production, but this capitalism is very much distorted and disarticulated. Moreover, the land question has not been fundamentally solved. No doubt, with the 'Green Revolution', some new class forces have emerged on the scene, but this so-called capitalist development has brought nothing except misery and resultant discontentment among the peasant masses, that too, on a massive scale. Despite some changes in the areas of the 'Green Revolution', no significant change has occurred in the semi-feudal relations of India as a whole.

What does 'big pro-capitalist landlords' mean? Does this mean feudal landlords who ally with capitalists or big landlords who favour capitalist relations of production in agriculture? The Maoist programme remains confused on this vital question. This convoluted conception of the agrarian scenario not only exposes the barrenness of the earlier naxalite understanding of the impossibility of capitalist development in Indian agriculture, but also reflect the non-serious approach of the Maoists in analysing the contemporary challenges arising out of imperialist penetration in agriculture in the post-liberalisation period. Such a view leads them to conclude in their *Strategy and Tactics of the Indian Revolution* that, 'the vast majority of India's population still...languish under semi-feudal conditions of existence', and posit 'the contradiction between feudalism and the broad masses' as the 'principal contradiction', which is to be resolved through 'armed agrarian revolution'/'protracted people's war'. What their view implies is that whatever be the extent of capitalist development in agriculture and no matter what the role of the state can be vis-à-vis protecting the peasantry from imperialist penetration today, they will continue to believe that India is semi-feudal and wage armed struggle against feudalism, because they decided so in 1967. Such obtuseness has made the Maoists practically irrelevant in contemporary peasant movements and kept them totally isolated from the peasant masses.

Misunderstanding the Indian Bourgeoisie

The Maoists' *Strategy and Tactics of the Indian Revolution* states, 'The present state machinery is the instrument of class repression, class exploitation and class rule of the comprador bureaucratic bourgeoisie and big landlords who subserve the imperialists.' That the 'comprador bureaucratic bourgeoisie' is identified by them with the big bourgeoisie is clear from their formulation that, 'the Indian state is the joint dictatorship of the big bourgeoisie-big landlord classes who serve imperialism'.

This makes a mockery of Mao himself. While elaborating on the character of the comprador bourgeoisie in China, Mao Zedong, in *Chinese Revolution and the Chinese Communist Party* (1939), had noted that 'The imperialist powers have established a network of comprador and merchant-usurer exploitation right across China, from the trading ports to the remote hinterland, and have created a comprador and merchant-usurer class in their service, so as to facilitate their exploitation of the masses of the Chinese peasantry and other sections of the people. The imperialist powers have made the feudal landlord class as well as the comprador class the main props of their rule in China.' A note to this document states: 'A comprador, in the original sense of the word, was the Chinese manager or the senior Chinese employee in a foreign commercial establishment. The compradors served foreign economic interests and had close connection with imperialism and foreign capital.' Mao Zedong further elaborated: 'There is a distinction between the comprador big bourgeoisie and the national bourgeoisie. The comprador big bourgeoisie is a class which directly serves the capitalists of the imperialist countries and is nurtured by them . . . different sections of the comprador big bourgeoisie owe allegiance to different imperialist powers.' In other words, the comprador bourgeoisie are virtual commission agents dependent on proceeds from buying and selling goods for various imperialist powers.

To see the Indian big bourgeoisie as comprador not only defies Mao Zedong's conception of the comprador bourgeoisie but also seeks to deny the vast industrial base of the Indian monopoly bourgeoisie extending to myriad sectors – steel, machinery, automobiles, textiles, telecommunications, oil, gas, petroleum, etc. The industrial base of the Indian big bourgeoisie, which existed even during the colonial period, witnessed exponential growth in the period since independence. This is borne out by the massive increase in its assets and wealth. The assets of the top 22 monopoly houses grew 500 times from around Rs 300 crore in 1957 to over Rs 1.5 lakh crore in 1997. While the Tatas and Birlas had assets of Rs 67 and Rs 63 crores respectively in 1947, the assets of the Ambani brothers, before they fell out in 2004–05 stood at Rs 1 lakh crores! Since then there has been a further increase in the wealth of the big bourgeoisie with the number of Indian dollar billionaires in the Forbes list increasing from 9 in 2004 to 49 in 2010. How can a bourgeoisie, which is merely a commission agent for various imperialist powers, continue to develop wealth and assets in such huge proportions?

The Maoists, like the naxalites in the 1960s, fail to see the large industrial base of the Indian big bourgeoisie, besides the control exercised by them over major part of the trade and service sectors, which creates interests of its own as a class. These interests and the concrete strengths and weaknesses of the Indian big bourgeoisie have historically determined its dual role of conflict and compromise vis-à-vis imperialism. Conflict arises out of clash of interests on control of indigenous markets and share in the world market. Collaboration and its tendency to increase with time are rooted in the relatively weak position of the Indian bourgeoisie as compared to the imperialist bourgeoisie, limitations imposed by its compromise with landlordism, its dependence for advanced technology on imperialist countries and lack of colonies that helped capital accumulation in the imperialist countries.

Given its relatively weaker position, the Indian bourgeoisie's relations with imperialism are no doubt unequal and dependent. The demise of socialism in the Soviet Union and the consequent strengthening of imperialism have also helped strengthen the trend towards increasing collaboration, particularly with US imperialism. However, increasing economic or strategic collaboration cannot be confused with being comprador. In the era of imperialist globalization, there is hardly any capitalist country in the world today whose bourgeoisie does not collaborate with imperialist finance capital, which while being based in the advanced capitalist countries, is basically transnational in character. Mixing up collaboration or dependence on imperialist finance with being comprador would lead to the absurd conclusion that the bourgeoisies, not only across all third world countries but also in the advanced capitalist countries have become universally comprador.

The Indian bourgeoisie has historically collaborated with imperialism and foreign finance capital in pursuit of the capitalist path of development in India since independence. This capitalist path acquired the specific character of state-sponsored development and planning during the phase when the strength of the big bourgeoisie was relatively weak and the existence of the socialist camp allowed relative autonomy vis-à-vis imperialism. With the advent of imperialist globalization and the collapse of the socialist camp in the late 1980s, along with the significant strengthening of the Indian big bourgeoisie by that time, a shift was made to a market oriented economy coupled with closer collaboration with imperialism. This was in keeping with the inherent duality of the Indian big bourgeoisie which arises out of its own class needs.

Given their characterization of India as a semi-colony since independence and its big bourgeoisie as comprador, the Maoists are out of their depths to explain the major shift that occurred in India's economic policy regime in 1991. While the Maoists' Programme does not explicitly admit this policy shift, it has been compelled to note in Para 16 that: 'Today, in India and all other backward countries, thousands of big imperialist MNCs and TNCs are openly operating. Imperialism is increasingly moving towards trampling under-foot the so-called sovereignty, in the neo-colonial type of semi-colonial countries through these policies. All kinds of restrictions are increasingly removed for the autocratic control, expansion and unrestricted exploitation of the imperialist finance capital. The so-called public sector, which was erected in the deceptive name of socialism to mislead the public opinion, is being offered to the comprador bourgeoisie and imperialist MNCs.'

There is a clear attempt to cover up utter theoretical confusion through too clever by half formulations. But if Indian independence in 1947 itself was 'fake in essence', how is its 'so-called sovereignty' being further 'trampl(ed) under-foot' by imperialism 'today'? What is a 'neo-colonial type of semi-colonial' country? How and why did 'all kinds of restrictions' on 'exploitation of the imperialist finance capital' that are now being 'increasingly removed', get imposed in the first place in a semi-colonial country with a comprador bourgeoisie? What stopped the 'so-called public sector' being 'offered' to the imperialist MNCs till 'today'? The Maoists would be hard put to provide answers to these questions because if the post-1991 phase is to be characterized as neocolonization of the Indian economy, then it puts paid to their thesis of India being a semi-colony since independence. Their basic problem, however, lies in dogmatically clinging to concepts like 'comprador bourgeoisie' and 'semi-colony', which have long been rendered irrelevant in the Indian context.

The complete misunderstanding of capitalist development in India, which permeates the Maoists' Programme, also leads to erroneous class analysis. For instance, they overrate the revolutionary potential of the non-big bourgeoisie which they consider to be 'politically very weak and vacillating', whose majority 'either remains neutral or participates in the revolution'. Similarly, they assert that 'the entire petty bourgeois class including even its right wing sails with the revolutionary tide'. All this betrays a failure to see the differentiation among the non-big bourgeoisie and the petty bourgeoisie engendered by capitalist development, especially in the post-liberalization phase. Sections of the non-big bourgeoisie and petty bourgeoisie have benefited from economic liberalization and form the support base for the neoliberal policies in India today. To count them as reliable allies of a revolutionary movement reflects naiveté.

The biggest gap in the class analysis of the Maoists, however, lies in their understanding of the working class itself, which is supposed to provide leadership to the revolution. There is no effort to study the condition of the working class in the urban areas, especially the intensified nature of their exploitation under the neoliberal regime through informalization and casualization of the workforce and the changes in the production processes. The fact that the Maoists put little premium on work among the urban working class is borne out by their inability to establish any trade unions till date. But how can a proletarian revolution be made without organizing a single member of the working class, especially when the urban working class population is growing by the day through migration? The Maoists refuse to engage with this vital question.

Blind Pursuit of the Chinese Path
Strategy and Tactics of the Indian Revolution states that, 'the path followed by the Chinese revolution is also applicable in semi-colonial, semi-feudal India due to basic similarities in conditions between India and pre-revolutionary China.' This blind pursuit of the Chinese path, which

primarily involves guerrilla struggle and protracted people's war, is the hallmark of the Maoist strategy. The Chinese path was first advocated in India by the Andhra Committee of the united CPI during the course of the Telangana armed struggle in 1948–51. The same period also saw sections of the CPI leadership advocating the Russian path of revolution based on insurrection in the towns and spreading to the countryside after capture of urban centres. This led to acute inner-Party con-flicts that were resolved with the adoption of the *Statement of Policy* that outlined the path of the Indian revolution along with the Party Programme at the Special Party Conference held at Calcutta in 1951.

This *Statement of Policy* had rejected any mechanical application of the Chinese or the Russian paths to India on the grounds that conditions in India were different from those in pre-revolutionary China and Russia. It had argued that the line favouring the Chinese path underestimated the role of the working class while the other view, advocating the Russian path with political general strike as the main strategic plank, underestimated the role of the peasantry in a predominantly rural country. Almost sixty years have elapsed since then. The development of capitalism during this period has led to rapid urbanization, exponential growth of the working class, especially in the urban informal sector, huge development of communications and accrual of much greater administrative and military prowess in the hands of the Indian state. The continued advocacy of the Chinese path by the Maoists in India totally ignores these changes, besides the obvious differences between pre-revolutionary China and contemporary India discussed in the sections above.

What underlies the supreme belief of the Maoists in armed struggle being the sole strategic cum tactical weapon for achieving revolution and their utter contempt for other forms of struggle is pure dogmatism. It renders them incapable of drawing any objective lessons even from their own experience. Their documents make no attempt to explain their inability over the past forty years to establish roots in areas other than those which are remote, hilly and forested, and where means of communications are backward. Neither are they willing to learn anything from the failure of similar guerilla wars in Peru and Phillippines or the move away from armed struggle by the Nepalese Maoists in the recent past. Rebutting this ostrich like tendency, Mao Zedong had observed in his classic, *On Contradictions*: 'Lenin meant just this when he said that the most essential thing in Marxism, the living soul of Marxism, is the concrete analysis of concrete conditions. Our dogmatists have violated Lenin's teachings; they never use their brains to analyse anything concretely, and in their writings and speeches they always use stereotypes devoid of content, thereby creating a very bad style of work in our Party.'

Mao had further observed, 'Our dogmatists are lazy-bones. They refuse to undertake any painstaking study of concrete things, they regard general truths as emerging out of the void, they turn them into purely abstract unfathomable formulas, and thereby completely deny and reverse the normal sequence by which man comes to know truth.' In sum, this is the basic problem with the theoretical foundations of the Maoists. By willfully ignoring objective reality, the Maoists ensure that they can never arrive at a correct strategy for revolution.

PERVERTED PRAXIS

The main content of the Maoists' People's War comprises of individual annihilation and terror directed at the police personnel, political rivals and petty state employees. This is accompanied by attacks on power and telecommunication towers, exploding railway tracks, burning down railway stations and government buildings and even blowing up schools and health centres. This is done through the aegis of small armed squads who carry out such murderous activities and vanish into the remoteness of their hideouts in the jungles and hills. They are nowhere to be seen when security forces unleash retaliatory repression on innocent peasants and tribals living in the areas where these actions were carried out.

The armed actions of the Maoists are hardly ever directed at annihilating big landlords, the sworn enemies of the agrarian revolution. Similarly individuals belonging to the 'comprador bureaucratic bourgeoisie' or top officials of MNCs are yet to feel the heat of their 'revolutionary retribution'. The Maoist leader Koteshwar Rao alias Kishanji has given a telling clue to explain this apparent ambiguity. In an interview with Tusha Mittal in *Tehelka* (November 13, 2009), he states that, 'We collect taxes from the corporates and big bourgeoisie, but it's not any different from the corporate sector funding the political parties.' This is candid indeed. Had he been more truthful he would have included big landlords, mining companies and forest contractors in the list of Maoist financers. Obviously, you do not bite the hand that feeds you!

Individual Annihilation and Terror

Individual annihilation and terror are employed by anarchists of all hues throughout the world. These tactics finds no sanction in Marxism-Leninism. The Communist International in its *Appeal to the Nationalists*, published as a supplement to *Vanguard* dated December 15, 1924, rejected such tactics in the following words: 'Violence is not per se an essential attribute of revolution. *Under the present state of society, political and social revolutions can hardly be expected to be bloodless and non-violent; but everything bloody and violent is not revolutionary.* A particular social system or political institution can never be overthrown by assassinating individuals upholding them' (emphasis added).

The same view was reflected in the *Statement of Policy* or the Tactical Line adopted by the CPI in 1951. It stated:

> Individual terrorism is directed against individuals of a class or system and is carried out by individuals or groups and squads. The individuals who act may be heroic and selfless and applauded or even invited by the people to act and the individuals against whom they act the most hated. Still such actions are not permissible in Marxism. And why? For the simple reason therein the masses are not in action. Therein, the belief is fostered that the heroes will do the job for the people. Therein, it fosters the belief that many more such actions will mean in sum total the annihilation of the classes or system. Ultimately it leads to passivity or inertia of the masses, stops their own action and development towards revolution and in the end results in defeat.

Communists would like revolutionary transformation with the least bloodshed. However, they also know from experience, at times extremely bitter, that the ruling classes never relinquish their power voluntarily but seek to defy the will of the people and reverse it by lawlessness and violence. This counter-revolutionary violence cannot be met by turning the other cheek but by determined mass revolutionary resistance that may involve violence as well. However, this cannot be equated with individual terrorism. There is a vast difference between violence that accompanies revolutionary upheavals and the individual annihilation and terror practiced by the Maoists in conditions where no mass insurrection exists. In the former case it is part of a process that involves huge sections of the masses mobilized in acute class struggle; in the latter only few individuals sans mass involvement.

What the tactics of individual annihilation means can be seen from the recent experiences of the tribal areas where the Maoists currently operate. The adivasis in the Bastar district of Chhattisgarh are caught between the vicious cycle of violence between the Maoists and the state-sponsored armed militia, Salva Judum, over the past few years. In Orissa, thousands of Christian tribals had to bear the brunt of the fascistic violence orchestrated by the Bajrang Dal, after the Maoists executed Vishwa Hindu Parishad leader Lakshmanananda Saraswati in August 2008 and fled from the scene. The general experience in states like Chhattisgarh, Jharkhand and Orissa shows that mindless violence by the Maoists and repression unleashed by the state using the pretext, invariably leads to a cycle of violence and counter-violence, shattering the lives and livelihoods of the poor tribals. In this violent milieu armed Maoist gangs get a free hand to indulge in extortion, robbery and mayhem. That such tactics do not lead to the advance of any revolutionary movement is clear as daylight. Yet the Maoists like the Bourbons of old refuse to learn or unlearn anything.

Poll Boycott and Dismissal of Democracy

The other major strategic cum tactical plank of the Maoists is that of poll boycott. This is justified in their *Strategy and Tactics of the Indian Revolution* on grounds that, 'in the concrete conditions of semi-colonial, semi-feudal India . . . the objective conditions permit the proletarian party to initiate and sustain armed struggle in the vast countryside. In the name of preparation for armed struggle, participation in election will only sabotage the revolutionary movement...participation in election neither helps in developing revolutionary class struggle, nor in enhancing democratic consciousness among the people. Rather it will only foster constitutional illusions'. Underlying this is the understanding that, 'In India, a revolutionary situation is existing...participation in parliament has no relation to the ebb and tide of revolution'.

The existence of a 'revolutionary situation' has a very specific connotation in Marxist-Leninist terminology. In essence it means a situation ripe for revolution. Keeping the rich experience of the Russian Revolution in mind, Lenin had in his 1920 work *Left Wing Communism, An Infantile Disorder*, outlined certain features of a situation ripe for revolution:

> we must not only ask ourselves whether we have convinced the vanguard of the revolutionary class, but also whether the historically effective forces of *all* classes – positively of all the classes of the given society without exception – are aligned in such a way that everything is fully ripe for the decisive battle; in such a way that (1) all the class forces hostile to us have become sufficiently entangled, are sufficiently at loggerheads with each other, have sufficiently weakened themselves in a struggle which is beyond their strength; that (2) all the vacillating, wavering, unstable intermediate elements – the petty bourgeoisie and the petty bourgeois democrats as distinct from the bourgeoisie – have sufficiently exposed themselves in the eyes of the people, have sufficiently disgraced themselves through their practical bankruptcy; and that (3) among the proletariat a mass sentiment in favour of supporting the most determined, supremely bold, revolutionary action against the bourgeoisie has arisen and begun vigorously to grow. The revolution is indeed ripe then . . .

Those who claim that a revolutionary situation, even remotely similar to the one described above exists in India today obviously have no touch with reality.

The Bolsheviks participated in elections to the bourgeois Parliament in Russia or the Constituent Assembly even in the period September to November 1917, which was one of a revolutionary crisis. Lenin justified this participation in *Left Wing Communism*:

> It is an absolutely incontestable and fully established historical fact that, in September–November 1917, the urban working class and the soldiers and peasants of Russia were, because of a number of special conditions, exceptionally well prepared to accept the Soviet system and to disband the most democratic of bourgeois parliaments. Nevertheless, the Bolsheviks did *not* boycott the Constituent Assembly, but took part in the elections both before *and*

after the proletariat conquered political power . . . these elections yielded exceedingly valuable (and to the proletariat, highly useful) political results . . .

By the Maoist logic, however, Lenin and the Bolshevik Party should be accused of revisionism!

In his speech on parliamentarianism at the 2nd Congress of the Communist International on August 2, 1920, Lenin rebutted the line of boycotting elections to bourgeois parliaments in the following words:

It has been claimed here that it is a waste of time to participate in the parliamentary struggle. Can one conceive of another institution in which all classes are interested as they are in parliament? This cannot be created artificially. If all classes are drawn into the parliamentary struggle, it is because the class interests and conflicts are reflected in parliament. If it were possible everywhere and immediately to bring about, let us say, a decisive general strike so as to overthrow capitalism at a single stroke, the revolution would have already taken place in a number of countries. But we must reckon with facts, and parliament is a scene of the class struggle.

In the same speech Lenin also accused those parties advocating boycott of elections of being afraid that they would not be able to compel their members of parliament to submit to their discipline. He traced the roots of this to the weakness of such parties in building a disciplined party.

Lenin was equally scathing in attacking right reformism and revisionism in his works like *State and Revolution* and *The Proletarian Revolution and the Renegade Kautsky*. He uncompromisingly opposed parliamentary cretinism that treated parliamentary struggle as primary, created illusions about bourgeois democracy and neglected the need to build extra-parliamentary struggles. Yet he did not advocate boycott of bourgeois parliaments.

The Maoists' understanding of bourgeois parliament and elections is entirely contrary to the ideas espoused by Lenin. They take the consciousness of the masses for granted and seek to impose the poll boycott line through terrorizing voters. That such tactics have always been a failure is borne out by the fact that polling percentage in general elections in India have remained between 55 to 62 per cent since the first parliamentary elections of 1952. In the 2009 Lok Sabha elections more than 58 per cent of the 714 million voters cast their vote.[5]

It is noteworthy that out of the 543 odd parliamentary constituencies across the country, the Election Commission had identified 79 (14.5 per cent) as 'naxal affected'. Despite this, the statement issued by the CPI (Maoist) Politbureau after the Lok Sabha polls falsely claims: 'People everywhere, and not merely in the areas under the influence of our Party, resorted to boycott as a form of protest and struggle. Overall, the majority of the Indian people showed a higher level of consciousness this time by rejecting the contesting candidates, the political parties, and the pseudo-democratic parliamentary system...More people stayed away from the polling booths than those who went to cast their votes.' It is difficult to argue with those who refuse to accept facts simply because they are inconvenient.

Maoists further claimed that 'boycott of polls has emerged as a dominant form of struggle in the elections held in April–May 2009 . . . rotten, stinking institution called Parliament had failed to create any interest whatsoever in the voter . . . (i)n Chhattisgarh, Bihar, Jharkhand, Maharashtra, MP, Orissa, and Kashmir, polling has been quite low with more than 50% of the voters rejecting the elections.' The actual polling percentages for these States were, Chhattisgarh: 55.30; Bihar: 44.84; Jharkhand: 51.52; Maharashtra: 50.76; Madhya Pradesh 50.87; Orissa: 65.34 and Jammu and Kashmir: 39.90. Thus, contrary to the Maoists' claim, every state where they have a presence (other than Bihar), registered over 50 per cent polling. As far as Jammu and Kashmir is concerned, the low polling had nothing to do with the Maoists but the two decades old separatist insurgency in the Kashmir valley.

The Maoists also make a most ludicrous claim regarding low polling in Mumbai symbolizing the success of their poll boycott campaign: 'The most publicized campaign by the NGOs, film actors, industrialists and eminent personalities in Mumbai saw only 43.52 per cent of the voters turning up, the lowest ever in the city.' Are we to believe that over 56 per cent of the electorate of Mumbai who did not vote – mostly comprising of the urban middle class and elites – were inspired by the revolutionary poll boycott call, despite the Maoists not having any presence in that city? It is a well known fact of Indian parliamentary democracy that the poorer and socially deprived sections have increasingly become keener participants in the election process, even as apathy and cynicism towards elections have grown in the middle and affluent classes. The Maoists' claim of enforcing a poll boycott in Mumbai is therefore not only laughable but also reflects a deeply skewed class perspective. It is noteworthy in this context that the states with a strong presence of the organized Left parties like West Bengal, Kerala and Tripura witnessed very high polling percentages of 80.67, 73.35 and 84.13 respectively.

The Maoists' dismissal of bourgeois democracy as being of no consequence for the working class and other toilers is at complete variance with the worldwide experience of the communists since the nineteenth century, in utilising parliament and legislatures as instruments to advance class struggle and to defend the democratic rights of the people. Although a form of class rule of the bourgeoisie, India's parliamentary system established after independence embodied a significant democratic advance for the people. It provided opportunities for the communists to fight for the interests of the workers and the peasantry, intervene in the affairs of the state to a certain extent and mobilise masses towards broader goals. The threats to parliamentary democracy in India has not come from the communists but from the ruling class parties like the Congress, which had imposed Emergency in the 1970s, and the BJP-led government's tenure, which had made attempts to rewrite the Indian Constitution at the behest of the Rashtriya Swayamsevak Sangh.

The Maoists' approach towards elections and parliamentary democracy, besides exposing their myopic vision regarding Indian society also betray a lack of comprehension of the problems of socialist construction in the twentieth century. Nowhere, either in their Programme or their *Strategy and Tactics of the Indian Revolution*, does one find any analysis of the actual experience of socialism, especially in the Soviet Union, in ensuring the democratic rights of the people. It is a well recognized fact that serious weaknesses in deepening democracy, violations of socialist legality, growth of bureaucratism and overlapping of the Party and the state were important factors behind alienation of the people from the Soviet state. These experiences neither merit any attention of the Maoists nor lead to any introspection. They prefer to remain caught in a time warp.

Distorted Understanding of the Nationality Question

In a multi-national country like India, a correct assessment and handling of the nationality question has a direct bearing on the unity of the working class and other toilers and hence the future of the democratic revolution. There is no single oppressor nationality in India. Instead, people belonging to all nationalities are victims of the class exploitation by India's bourgeois-landlord ruling classes. Unfortunately, the naxalites have never understood this simple truth and had lent their active support to secessionist and divisive movements like those for Khalistan and independent Assam. Their flawed characterization of the Indian ruling classes as comprador and of India as a semi-colony of different imperialist powers had provided them the basis to justify the right to self determination or secession of different nationalities from the Indian Union.

The Maoists remain faithful to this disruptive line. Thus, *Strategy and Tactics of the Indian Revolution* states, 'we must make a distinction between the nationalities of the North East and Kashmir . . . and those in other states [as] the former have never considered themselves to be part of India . . . [and] the ruling classes . . . have continued their occupation of the territories of these nationalities'. They pledge 'complete and unflinching support to the demand for secession of these nationalities as long as their struggle is directed against our common enemies.' Kashmir and the North East are areas where the demand for secession is the strongest. However, support for secession is not limited to Kashmir and the North East alone. This is borne out by their general formulation that, 'If, however, the entire people of (a) nationality insist on seceding, we must not oppose it'. In other words, their position in essence remains the same as that of earlier naxalism, i.e., sanction to secession based on a mechanical application of the right to self-determination of different nationalities.

Marxist-Leninists have never considered the right to self-determination and secession as an absolute right. Such issues have to be decided keeping the concrete case in mind. However, there is one overarching principle that has guided their decisions in this regard, namely, does it serve the interest of the working class movement or not. The writings of Marx, Lenin, Stalin and other communist revolutionaries provide any number of examples of the application of this criterion in dealing with different demands for self-determination.

Thus in the 1840s Marx supported the Polish and Hungarian national movements while opposing those of the Czechs and the South Slavs. Marx's support to the former was guided not just by the fact that they represented oppressed nationalities but also because the Polish and Hungarian movements were directed against the absolutism of the Russian and Austrian Empires, for political democracy which was of vital interest to the European working class at that time. He opposed the Czech and South Slav movements because this would amount to indirect support to Tsarism, which was the most dangerous enemy of the revolutionary movement in Europe.[6] Lenin wrote in *The Discussion on Self-Determination Summed Up* (1916), that 'The various demands of democracy, including self determination, are not an absolute, but a small part of the general democratic (now general socialist) world movement. In individual concrete cases, the part may contradict the whole; if so it must be rejected.'

What would secession of any state from the Indian Union today imply for the working class movement in India? This should be a touchstone for judging the demands for self-determination of various nationalities from a Marxist-Leninist standpoint. Weakening of the unity between the different nationalities in India would not only weaken the Indian state vis-à-vis imperialism but also adversely impact on the unity of the working people. The toilers of the seceding nationality will go out of the pale of the pan-Indian movement, thereby weakening both themselves and the general movement of the Indian working class. The case of Kashmir is especially pertinent. Its secession can only mean either merger into Pakistan or setting up of an independent state. Merger into Pakistan will mean becoming part of a more regressive set up, where feudal elements are stronger, the ruling classes are totally subservient to US imperialism and democracy itself is on a fragile footing. The option of independent Kashmir is also untenable. A landlocked entity with a strategic location, but with few resources, would inevitably land up becoming a client of imperialism. It will provide US imperialism a base to unleash its machinations against all neighbouring countries – India, China, Pakistan, Afghanistan and the Central Asian republics. Such a dispensation cannot be very liberating for the Kashmiri people.

Opposition to the demand for secession, however, does not circumscribe the responsibility of a Communist Party to fight for genuine demands of different nationalities for autonomy and self-rule, while steering clear of any form of national chauvinism and secessionist trends. This alone can help advance the cause of different nationalities as part of the united struggle of the Indian people for democratic advance. The Maoists, however, are not only supportive of all secessionist demands but also provide unequivocal support to all demands for separate statehood, whether in Telangana, the North East or elsewhere. That this undermines the linguistic organization of the States and that the vivisection of existing states into smaller entities will further undermine federalism and strengthen central authority to the detriment of the interests of the states and their people, is of no concern to them. It is notable that while being indiscriminately supportive of all separate statehood demands, the Maoists are practically on the same page with the RSS, which has never been comfortable with the linguistic organization of states which accorded the state with a federal and democratic character.

In *Strategy and Tactics of the Indian Revolution*, the Maoists speak of 'other forms of oppression by a certain dominant nation (oppression by Bengalis over Assamese and over other nationalities of the North East; the oppression by the Assamese over the small nationalities in the state of Assam such as the Bodos, Karbis, Mishings, etc.)'. They further elaborate that 'appropriate forms of struggle and organization should be evolved to fight every manifestation of national oppression taking all care, at the same time, to bring the people of the particular nationality out of national aloofness and to promote a spirit of international solidarity among them.' How can solidarity be built among the various nationalities if the basic premise is that every nationality is guilty of 'national oppression' in some way or the other? Devoid of any proper Marxist understanding of the nationality question, the Maoists eventually land up tailing each and every divisive demand, which only serves to widen the rifts among people and weaken the bonds between various nationalities in India.

BLIND ANIMOSITY TOWARDS ORGANIZED LEFT

The organized Left has always been the special target of murderous attacks by left adventurists since the late 1960s. The Maoists have carried this tradition to newer heights in recent years. While these attacks are mostly occurring in West Bengal where the CPI (M)-led Left Front runs the state government, it is not confined to that state. This is borne out by the murders of two CPI (M) activists in Bhadrachalam district of Andhra Pradesh, the killing of a CPI (M) worker in Kanker, Chhattisgarh, and the abduction and killing of a CITU leader in Kalta, Orissa, by Maoist gangs in the past few months. Their murderous campaign against the CPI (M) has been most acute in the West Medinipur district of West Bengal and other two districts of the state bordering Jharkhand, whose jungles provide safe haven to the Maoist death squads. Their murder spree was preceded by Maoist support to Trinamul Congress goons in Nandigram that led to killing of several CPI (M) supporters and rendered thousands of them homeless. Then came their abortive attempt to assassinate the West Bengal Chief Minister on November 2, 2008, when he was returning after the inauguration of a steel plant in West Medinipur district.

The Maoist cadres who had executed the assassination attempt had taken shelter in the Lalgarh area of West Medinipur. The police investigations into the attempt on the Chief Minister's life saw a few instances of excesses on the local tribals during its course. Taking note of this, the West Bengal government transferred the policemen involved, besides ensuring the release of some of those arrested and payment of compensation to those injured. However, using the discontent created, the Maoists set up a People's Committee against Police Atrocities (PCPA) and announced that the state administration would not be allowed into Lalgarh. All attempts of the district administration to reach an amicable settlement were thwarted by the PCPA and the area was kept under blockade from mid-November 2008. This was followed by a vicious campaign to kill CPI (M) cadres and supporters and terrorize the people into submission. The Maoists celebrated this as the revival of the spirit of Naxalbari and justified such murders on the plea that the CPI (M) represents a 'social-fascist' force! Over 100 CPI (M) activists and supporters have been killed by the Maoists in this district since then along with some activists of other tribal organizations and parties like the Bharat Jakat Majhi Marwa Sangathan and the Jharkhand Party (Naren). Most of the slain victims were agricultural workers, tribal peasants, small shopkeepers, students or other rural poor. In many cases they were the sole bread earners of their families.

The Maoists have been unable to build any mass movement against the CPI (M) in West Medinipur or the neighbouring districts of Purulia and Bankura, which have a significant tribal population. Their failure arises from the fact that the CPI (M) has deep roots in these tribal inhabited regions based on its record of peasant struggles since the 1960s and the benefits accruing to the people there from land reforms pursued by the Left Front government since 1977. While the tribal areas of West Bengal continue to suffer from relative backwardness as compared to the rest of the state, the condition of the tribal people in that region is better compared to the tribal areas of Jharkhand, Chhattisgarh or Orissa. Out of the 4.56 lakh hectares of land vested and redistributed in West Bengal upto November 2009, over 94000 hectares have been redistributed in the West Medinipur district alone, which is the highest for any district in the state. Over 1.70 lakh tribal peasants have benefited from land redistribution in the West Medinipur district and another 24000 odd recorded as bargadars (sharecroppers) securing their tenancy rights. Further details of land redistribution in the tribal inhabited districts of West Bengal are provided in the tables (facing page).[7]

Despite the Lalgarh blockade and the Maoist poll boycott call during the Lok Sabha elections held in May 2009, the CPI (M) candidate won from the Jhargram (ST reserved) constituency, where Lalgarh is located, by securing 5.45 lakh votes (nearly 57% of total votes polled) and with a margin of 2.9 lakh votes over the runner-up candidate from the Congress. The Left Front candidates also won with convincing margins in the adjacent Lok Sabha constituencies of Purulia and Bankura which have a significant proportion of tribal population. Coming at a time when the Left suffered electoral reverses elsewhere in the state, this only underlines the continued mass support behind the CPI (M) and the Left Front in these tribal areas.

Following the Lok Sabha elections, joint operations were launched by the state and central security forces in Lalgarh, which ended the blockade without any resistance and zero casualties. The Maoists fled into the jungles on the Jharkhand border, but have continued their murderous strikes from there till date.

The Maoists claim to be 'liberators' of the people. The state of affairs in Lalgarh during the period of their blockade exposes the real nature of this so-called 'liberation'. Ration shops, public works, schools and health centres were closed down. The peasants could not harvest their rice crop or sow potato and other winter vegetables because of the

AREA OF VESTED AGRICULTURAL LAND DISTRIBUTED AND NUMBER OF BENEFICIARIES (as on 30th November 2009)

State / District	Area of land distributed (in hectares)	Number of beneficiaries (persons)		
		Scheduled castes	Scheduled tribes	Total
West Bengal (all districts)	456490	1102757	548719	2988565
West Medinipur	94812	205259	170651	669904
Bankura	26069	93015	37308	180013
Purulia	29779	32313	32842	93274

RECORDING OF BARGADARS (as on 30th November 2009)

State / District	Scheduled castes		Scheduled tribes		Total	
	No. of beneficiaries	Area (hectares)	No. of beneficiaries	Area (hectares)	No. of beneficiaries	Area (hectares)
West Bengal (all districts)	473119	149842	166869	63601	1536831	455781
West Medinipur	41001	6286	24464	5024	151434	31471
Bankura	31912	7478	12533	3370	116853	27179
Purulia	3409	1549	2411	816	9344	3445

Source: Land and Land Reforms Department, published in Statistical Appendix, *Economic Review 2009-10*, Government of West Bengal.

hefty fines and taxes imposed on them by the Maoists.[8] Students were not able to attend schools or take part in board examinations. Following the entry of the security forces in Lalgarh and the fleeing of the Maoists, development work has resumed in full steam. The Left Front government in the state has immediately focussed upon improving employment generation through the NREGA, distribution of BPL cards, opening medical camps, drinking water supply and providing old age pension to the people of the Lalgarh and the adjoining area affected by Maoist violence. People have responded positively to these measures.

The unabated Maoist violence against the CPI (M), especially in West Medinipur, is interpreted by some commentators as a reflection of alienation of the CPI (M) from the people. This is a fallacious argument. In fact the persistence of these attacks till date shows that the ties of the CPI (M) with the tribal people have not weakened and their supporters are unwilling to abandon the Party even in the face of death and brutality. Had the CPI (M) been abandoned by the people, such attacks would not have been necessary. Maoist activities in West Medinipur and elsewhere in West Bengal has mainly been sustained through the open political and logistical support of the Trinamul Congress, the right reactionary opposition to the Left Front. During the Maoist blockade in Lalgarh, the Trinamul Congress supremo Mamata Banerjee was allowed to visit the place on February 4, 2009. She shared the platform with Chhatradhar Mahato, PCPA leader and brother of Shashadhar Mahato, the Maoist who led the attack on the West Bengal Chief Minister, and expressed support for their cause. She has repeatedly opposed the deployment of security forces in Lalgarh claiming that there are no Maoists there and that those being called Maoists are none other than CPI (M) people.

This nexus between the Maoists and the Trinamul was thoroughly exposed by Maoist commander Koteshwar Rao in an interview to the Bengali daily *Ananda Bazar Patrika* on October 4, 2009, where he stated that the Maoists would like to see Mamata Banerji as the next Chief Minister of Bengal. He justified his position by hailing her capacity to rise above class interest and adopt pro-people positions! This gives the game away – the 'revolutionary' Maoists are willing to become handmaiden of right wing and reactionary forces to satiate their psychotic hatred towards the CPI (M). This is the inevitable denouement of pseudo-revolutionary petty bourgeois adventurism.

While one hears shrill voices of certain sections of intellectuals denouncing the presence of security forces in Lalgarh as state repression, their deafening silence about the gruesome killings of CPI (M) cadres by Maoist hit men, the terror let loose by them and their heinous attempt to assassinate the Chief Minister of a democratically elected government, speaks volumes about the hypocritical concern of such intellectuals for democracy and human rights.

CONCLUSION

The programmatic understanding of the CPI (Maoist) betrays their inability to understand contemporary imperialism and accounts for their refusal to fight against concrete manifestations of imperialist machinations. Their characterization of *jehadis* as anti-imperialist and their unwillingness to see the anti-imperialist content of progressive movements in Latin America is a recipe for distorting and derailing today's anti-imperialist struggle. Their characterization of the Indian state and society is not only a gross travesty of facts but also seeks to conceal from the people the true nature of class exploitation and the strength of the Indian ruling classes. Their artificial assessment about the existence of a revolutionary situation in India today leads the Maoists to practice individual annihilation and mindless terror. This invites state repression, the brunt of which is borne by innocents, which in turn severely harms the possibilities of organizing them under the red flag for a long time to come. It also provides fertile ground to reactionary forces to rally these people behind them. The Maoist slogan of poll boycott and their contempt towards parliamentary democracy in India, also dovetails with the attempts of the ruling classes to undermine democratic institutions and prevent the working people from using them in their own interest.

Maoists' blind hatred for the organized Left and its biggest contingent, the CPI (M), reflected in murderous attacks on its members and sympathizers and their willingness to ally with right reactionary forces to achieve these ends, warms the hearts of both imperialism and the Indian ruling classes. In sum, the CPI (Maoist) represents nothing more than a left sectarian and anarchist force, which disrupts and discredits the Left and harms the interests of the democratic peoples' movement. They need to be thoroughly exposed before the people and combated ideologically and politically.

NOTES

[1] Their similar role in Andhra Pradesh was laid bare by P. Sundarayya, former General Secretary of the CPI (M), in his booklet *Congress (I)-Naxalite Gang Up: Attacks on CPI (M) Workers in Warangal.*

[2] See CPI (Maoist) Politbureau statement, *Post-Election Situation – Our Tasks*, June 2009.

[3] See Sumanta Banerji, 'Critiquing the Programme of Action of the Maoists', *Economic & Political Weekly*, November 14, 2009.

[4] As per the NSS 61st Round, 26 per cent of India's rural households comprised agricultural labourers in 2004–05.

[5] All figures of polling percentages are from the Election Commission of India. See http://eci.nic.in.

[6] See J.V. Stalin, 'The National Question', in *Foundations of Leninism*, 1953.

[7] All data on land redistribution are from the Land and Land Reforms Department, Government of West Bengal.

[8] For details, see *The Truth Behind the Violence in West Bengal*, AIDWA Publication, December 2009.

The Tragedy of 'Maoism'

Nilotpal Basu

The activities of the Indian Maoists have drawn public attention in recent times. It is the violence that they have unleashed, rather than their political cause, which has come into the focus of debate. The Union Government has characterized them as India's 'biggest internal security threat'. According to the Union Home Ministry, 3,338 persons have died in 7,806 incidents involving naxalite violence between 2004 and 2008. 908 persons have died in 2,258 incidents in 2009. The Union Government has also launched a security offensive along with the concerned state governments in the Maoist infested areas.

For those in the Left, however, there is a need to understand the ideology and politics of the CPI (Maoist), which is the fountainhead of their campaign of violence. It is especially important to examine their claim that their violent activities are inevitable in order to usher in a revolutionary transformation of Indian society. Since the Maoists claim to be a Communist force, let us examine their politics from a Marxist-Leninist viewpoint.

Marx wrote in the opening lines of *The Eighteenth Brumaire of Louis Bonaparte*: 'Hegel remarks somewhere that all great world-historic facts and personages appear, so to speak, twice. He forgot to add: the first time as tragedy, the second time as farce.' Marx elaborates on this understanding of history in the following words:

> Men make their own history, but they do not make it as they please; they do not make it under self-selected circumstances, but under circumstances existing already, given and transmitted from the past . . . The social revolution of the nineteenth century cannot take its poetry from the past but only from the future. It cannot begin with itself before it has stripped away all superstition about the past. The former revolutions required recollections of past world history in order to smother their own content. The revolution of the nineteenth century must let the dead bury their

dead in order to arrive at its own content. There the phrase went beyond the content – here the content goes beyond the phrase.[1]

Thus while envisioning a revolutionary project within the Marxist framework, it is important to 'arrive at its own content', most importantly forming a vision for the future rather than remaining 'superstitious' about the past. Moreover, the content of the revolutionary project should shape its form; not the other way round. This insight is central to our examination of the Maoists in India today.

MAO ZEDONG'S CONTRIBUTION

For revolutionaries across the world who try to apply Marxism-Leninism in the specific conditions prevailing in different societies, Mao Zedong will always be regarded as one of the greatest revolutionaries of the twentieth century. The Communist Party of China (CPC) under the leadership of Deng Xiaoping, whom the Indian Maoists consider as the protagonist of capitalist restoration in China, also reverently referred to Mao as the 'principal architect' of the great Chinese Revolution, even as they made a critical assessment of his overall contribution including the errors committed during the Cultural Revolution. But to the Maoists, Mao Zedong is beyond any criticism. They attach an almost divine infallibility to him and seek to emulate in Indian conditions, his analysis, strategies and tactics during the Chinese revolution. This is not only contrary to the essence of the Marxist understanding of history but goes against the method applied by Mao himself.

How did Mao Zedong develop the theory and practice of the Chinese revolution? Let us draw from Mao's writings themselves. In December 1939, Mao along with other leaders of the CPC drafted a textbook for the Party cadres and Chinese people titled *The Chinese Revolution and the Chinese Communist Party*. In this seminal work, Mao proceeded to understand the evolution of the Chinese society, the Chinese nation and the extant semi-colonial and semi-feudal relations in the backdrop of which the CPC had undertaken the task of carrying out a new democratic revolution. Following a comprehensive analysis of the Chinese society and state, its class composition and the nature of contradictions between the classes, the strategy and tactics of the Chinese revolution were worked out. The document explains the phenomenon of 'imperialist penetration of China – the blood-stained picture of feudal China being reduced to semi-feudal, semi-colonial and colonial China' and how that has led to 'transforming a feudal into a semi-feudal society, and on the other, imposed their [imperialist powers'] ruthless rule on China, reducing an independent country to a semi-colonial and colonial country'.[2] Proceeding from such an analysis, the following conclusion is derived:

> The contradiction between imperialism and the Chinese nation and the contradiction between feudalism and the great masses of the people are the basic contradictions in modern Chinese society. Of course, there are others, such as the contradiction between the bourgeoisie and the proletariat and the contradictions within the reactionary ruling classes themselves. But the contradiction between imperialism and the Chinese nation is the principal one. These contradictions and their intensification must inevitably result in the incessant growth of revolutionary movements. The great revolutions in modern and contemporary China have emerged and grown on the basis of these basic contradictions.[3]

It is noteworthy that while developing these ideas, Mao and his comrades were making significant departures from the dominant revolutionary ideas of their time, which were greatly shaped by the proletarian revolution in Russia and propagated by the Comintern as the only possible revolutionary path. Rather than adhering to the path of Russian revolution as a dogma or 'superstition', the CPC under Mao's leadership concluded that the Chinese revolution should be of a new democratic type, where the main task will be to achieve national liberation and elimination of landlordism. The CPC was clear about the form of the revolutionary struggle. Mao states:

> In the face of such enemies, the Chinese revolution cannot be other than protracted and ruthless. With such powerful enemies, the revolutionary forces cannot be built up and tempered into a power capable of crushing them except over a long period of time. With enemies who so ruthlessly suppress the Chinese revolution, the revolutionary forces cannot hold their own positions, let alone capture those of the enemy, unless they steel

themselves and display their tenacity to the full. It is therefore wrong to think that the forces of the Chinese revolution can be built up in the twinkling of an eye, or that China's revolutionary struggle can triumph overnight. In the face of such enemies, the principal means or form of the Chinese revolution must be armed struggle, not peaceful struggle. *For our enemies have made peaceful activity impossible for the Chinese people and have deprived them of all political freedom and democratic rights.*[4] (Emphasis added.)

Mao had also emphasized that military tactics, adopted at a time when 'peaceful activity' has been rendered impossible, is an extension of the political strategy and therefore the form of armed struggle is subordinate to the political content of the revolution:

[S]tressing armed struggle does not mean abandoning other forms of struggle; on the contrary, armed struggle cannot succeed unless coordinated with other forms of struggle. And stressing the work in the rural base areas does not mean abandoning our work in the cities and in the other vast rural areas which are still under the enemy's rule; on the contrary, without the work in the cities and in these other rural areas, our own rural base areas would be isolated and the revolution would suffer defeat. Moreover, the final objective of the revolution is the capture of the cities, the enemy's main bases, and this objective cannot be achieved without adequate work in the cities.[5]

Mao had thus underlined the importance of 'other forms of struggle' and 'work in the cities' along with armed struggle. That Mao's revolutionary vision was deeply democratic and not marked by any one-sided and slanted approach against bourgeois democratic institutions can also be seen from his writings like *The Tasks of the Chinese Communist Party in the Period of Resistance to Japan* (1937). Here he emphasized that a 'democratic reconstruction of the political system' was vital, along with a 'genuinely democratic government', freedom of speech, assembly and association, in order to unite and mobilize the Chinese people against Japanese imperialism.

China must at once start democratic changes in the two following respects. First, in the matter of the political system, the reactionary Kuomintang dictatorship of one party and one class must be changed into a democratic government based on the co-operation of all parties and all classes. In this respect, a start should be made by changing the undemocratic procedures for electing and convening the national assembly, and by holding democratic elections to the assembly and ensuring freedom in the conduct of its meetings, after which it will be necessary to go on to framing and adopting a truly democratic constitution, convening a truly democratic parliament, and electing a genuinely democratic government that will carry out genuinely democratic policies.[6]

Mao has also elaborated in other writings how the conclusion that the CPC would wage protracted armed struggle was arrived upon on the basis of the concrete realities prevailing in China during that period. Mao had emphasized the specificities of the Chinese situation, which made armed struggle necessary as well as plausible, for achieving the revolutionary goal. Mao explains in *Why is it that Red Political Power can Exist in China?* (1928) that:

it cannot occur in any imperialist country or in any colony under direct imperialist rule, but can only occur in China which is economically backward, and which is semi-colonial and under indirect imperialist rule. For this unusual phenomenon can occur only in conjunction with another unusual phenomenon, namely, war within the White regime. It is a feature of semi-colonial China that, since the first year of the Republic (1912) the various cliques of old and new warlords have waged incessant wars against one another, supported by imperialism from abroad and by the comprador and landlord classes at home. Such a phenomenon is to be found in none of the imperialist countries nor for that matter in any colony under direct imperialist rule, but only in a country like China which is under indirect imperialist rule. Two things account for its occurrence, namely, a localized agricultural economy (not a unified capitalist economy) and the imperialist policy of marking off spheres of influence in order to divide and exploit. The prolonged splits and wars within the White regime provide a condition for the emergence and persistence of one or more small Red areas under the leadership of the Communist Party amidst the encirclement of the White regime.[7]

These references to Mao's writings during the course of the revolutionary movement in China show how the strategy and tactics of the CPC evolved out of a correct analysis of the concrete situation prevailing in China during that period. If one has to grasp the essence of Mao's revolutionary contributions, it lies in the creative application of Marxism-Leninism in the concrete conditions prevailing in a society. The so-called 'Maoists', unfortunately, make the cardinal mistake of seeking to merely emulate the form of the Chinese revolution, i.e. armed struggle, without grasping the basic content of Mao's thought; which lies in studying the concrete conditions and analyzing the social contradictions correctly in order to strategize for a revolution.

WHAT IS 'MAOISM'?

By blindly imitating the specific path of the Chinese revolution under Mao's leadership, Indian 'Maoists' in fact undermine the very contribution of that great revolution. The Chinese Revolution happened at a time in history when national liberation struggles were emerging victorious across the third world in the wake of the great victory over fascism led by the Soviet Union. India's independence from colonial rule was also attained during the same period. These momentous developments had changed the alignment of political forces in the aftermath of the Second World War. The Indian Maoists, however, continue to believe in what the Naxalbari movement propounded, that Indian independence is fake and that India continues to be a semi-colonial state. Revolutionaries, whose hallmark is to usher in change, cannot remain oblivious to big changes at the global and national level and fail to assimilate their implications.

The CPI (ML) which emerged during the Naxalbari movement articulated unrealistic slogans, including, 'China's Chairman is our Chairman' and 'Chinese path is our path'. Contrast this to the opposition of Mao himself to the general line of Communist International in so far as China was concerned. It was Mao who asserted, and correctly so, that the Chinese revolution could not follow the same trajectory as in Russia.

Similarly, the Communists in India have to chart their own road to the revolution on the basis of a concrete analysis of Indian conditions. Wholesale borrowing from the methods followed by the Chinese Communist Party before the revolution in China in the name of 'Maoism' is against the very grain of Mao Zedong Thought. In fact, the very notion of 'Maoism' is a misplaced one. This was made clear by the Communist Party of China itself: 'Mao Zedong Thought, the product of the integration of the universal principles of Marxism-Leninism with the *concrete practice* of the Chinese revolution.'[8] To try and replicate the path of the Chinese revolution in India, lock, stock and barrel, is nothing but a denial of the Indian realities.

The basic problem with the conceptual framework of Indian 'Maoism' lies in the inability to come to grips with the changing situation and grasping the concrete realities in the society where they are working. The Maoists cling to the basic analysis of the Indian state as it was propounded forty years ago in the CPI (ML) programme in the wake of the Naxalbari movement. This analysis is based on an understanding that Indian independence is fake and formal with Indian rulers subservient to an imperialist order which is itself in a state of imminent collapse. This led the CPI (ML) to believe that an armed struggle involving the rural areas to 'encircle' the cities will deliver the 'revolution' in quick time. Slogans like 'decade of the seventies – a decade of liberation' appeared in naxalite wall writings on the streets of Kolkata. That the objective experience did not vindicate such an assessment ought to have triggered some degree of introspection. That was not to be. Attempts at reviewing and correcting their theoretical framework, rather than leading to more clarity, only resulted in utter confusion and splintering of the CPI (ML) into myriad factions and groups.

The naxalite characterization of the Indian bourgeoisie as 'comprador' or 'comprador bureaucratic bourgeoisie' is the basic source of its errors. A thesis adopted at the Sixth Congress of the Communist International (1928) states the following:

> The national bourgeoisie in these colonial countries does not adopt a uniform attitude in relation to imperialism. A part of this bourgeoisie, more especially the trading bourgeoisie, directly serves the interests of imperialist capital (the so-called comprador

bourgeoisie). In general, it more or less consistently defends the anti-national imperialist point of view directed against the whole nationalist movement, in common with the feudal allies of imperialism and the more highly paid native officials.[9]

Moreover, in a footnote it is further explained that 'comprador' means 'native merchants, engaged in trade with imperialist centres, whose interests are in continuation of imperialist exploitation. They act as agents for exploiting the masses in the colonial countries'. Thus this is a bourgeoisie that does not seek independent development of capitalism in its country. It is a mere puppet of imperialism. Such a bourgeoisie, therefore, does not command a social base of its own.

To characterize the Indian big bourgeoisie as 'comprador' is to grossly misunderstand the character of the ruling classes. The Indian ruling classes consist of an alliance between the bourgeoisie and the landlords, led by the big bourgeoisie. The big bourgeoisie, in turn, increasingly collaborates with imperialism and international finance capital. At the same time, it must be recognized that the Indian big bourgeoisie has a dual character. On the one hand, being a part of the world capitalist system and seeking to develop capitalism in India, it collaborates with imperialism and international finance capital. On the other hand, in order to preserve its economic domain from being encroached upon by global capital, it also has conflicts with imperialism. Such conflicts, however, get resolved not by confrontation but through compromise, pressure and bargain. This dual character finds its most visible expression in the economic and foreign policies of the government. The phase of neoliberal globalization has seen the accentuation of the collaborationist role of the Indian big bourgeoisie.

Without understanding the complexity of the process of capitalist development in India and mechanically presuming an exact resemblance with pre-revolutionary China has resulted in the Maoists remaining clueless in explaining what has happened in the decades since independence. Heavy industry and infrastructure like railways, power, telecommunications and technology in advanced areas like space, nuclear, knowledge-based industries like bio-technology and information technology – these have developed in India as part of the overall development of capitalism since independence. The indigenous capacities built over the years are unthinkable had it been spearheaded by a 'comprador bureaucratic bourgeoisie'. The wealth and assets of the Indian bourgeoisie have grown to such an extent that the Indian bourgeoisie now rates as among the most powerful and influential within the developing economies. The present era of globalization has seen the Indian bourgeoisie acquiring companies and assets abroad. To theorize the Indian bourgeoisie as 'comprador', therefore, not only amounts to underestimating its strength and social base, but to grossly misconstrue the Indian realities.

MINDLESS MILITARISM

Just as their theoretical understanding about capitalist development in India is totally out of line with the realities, the practice of the Maoists has little to do with people's livelihood and socio-economic justice. There are a large number of issues which are connected with the forest rights of tribals and their access to forest produce, on which the organized Left and other progressive and democratic forces wage struggle. These are of no interest to the Maoists. Far from participating in democratic struggles against the changes in the mining laws of the country – which has led to the indiscriminate entry of big capital in the tribal dominated areas resulting in displacement and exploitation of the tribals and other forest dwellers – the Maoists only indulge in violence in the name of armed revolution. The assumption is that the tribal people can only be mobilized under the slogan of a 'protracted people's war' and policy changes can only take place after the 'revolutionary' government is established.

Similarly, despite their shrill anti-imperialist rhetoric, when it comes to taking up issues and mobilizing people against imperialist-dictated policies, there is a deafening silence. The Maoists have never spoken out against the disastrous impact of financial liberalization, privatization of the public sector and heightened speculative activities in the economy in the post-liberalization era. Neither have they raised their voice against the withdrawal of state support to peasant agriculture, which has been the main reason for the severe agrarian crisis in the country causing farmers' suicide.

The cult of the gun, the firepower of the guerrillas and the discourse on military tactics has completely overwhelmed the Maoists. Mao himself warned against the dangers of mindless militarism on several occasions. The biggest danger of such mindless militarism lies in the fact that they provoke repression from the state which not only eliminates the so-called 'revolutionaries' but also exposes innocent rural poor to repression, demoralizes them and impacts adversely on their potential to organize and fight for their rights. The rural poor continue to remain victims of exploitation and depredation. A glaring instance of this phenomenon can be seen in Chhattisgarh, where the tribals today are caught in a vicious cycle of violence and counter-violence by the Maoists and the state-sponsored militia, Salva Judum. In the process, the Maoists manage to disrupt the emergence of a strong democratic movement which raises the level of revolutionary consciousness of the poor and the exploited.

What happens as a result of such mindless militarism is evident from the large material which has now been brought out in the public domain, by those who had been fellow travelers of the People's War Group based in Andhra Pradesh. Human rights activist Dr. K. Balagopal, who passed away recently, had brought out in graphic detail the degeneration of the Maoists in his Telegu essay *'Cheekati Konalu'* or 'The Darker side of the Naxalite Movement'. He described several heinous and ghastly acts of the PWG, bringing out their sadistic character which ought to be alien to a revolutionary movement. In order to make immediate tactical and military gains, the PWG has not flinched from having unholy alliances with landlords and other ruling class elements.

In their document 'Post Election Situation and our Tasks' issued after the 2009 Lok Sabha elections, the Maoists have admitted that 'in the last government, where it had a smaller number of seats, the Congress was totally dependent on its various allies in order to continue in power and the Left too exerted some amount of pressure on Manmohan Singh government for almost four years.' And they conclude, 'the [election] result has given scope for the UPA government to enact more draconian legislation'. Despite this, they started intensifying their attack in the post-election period against the Left while embracing the second largest component of the UPA government – the Trinamul Congress! Eventually, they have ended up becoming the armed mercenaries of the Trinamul in the forest areas of West Bengal bordering Jharkhand. This gang up with the right reactionary forces against the CPI (M)-led Left Front completely exposes their opportunism and shows how they are divorced from any class outlook.

QUESTION OF DEMOCRACY

Communists the world over have vigorously debated and engaged with the question of democracy, especially after the collapse of the Soviet Union. In India, parties like the CPI (M) had been in the forefront of the defence of democratic rights during the Emergency and have struggled for secularism and democracy in the face of depredations by the communal-fascist forces. They have also assessed the deficiencies that existed in the Soviet Union, which contributed in no small measure to its eventual collapse. The CPI (M) in its 14th Congress document titled *On Certain Ideological Issues* (1992) notes:

> . . . as the socialist system and the state consolidated and the correlation of class forces changed in its favour, opportunities for widening democracy and new initiatives opened up. Unfortunately, incorrect assessments of the reality led to the earlier methods of running the state machinery being carried over into the subsequent period. This led not only to the failure to realise the full potential of widening and deepening socialist democracy and popular people's participation but also to distortions such as growing bureaucratism, violation of socialist legality and suppression of individual freedom and liberty. The movement to higher phases of the form of the dictatorship of the proletariat implies the progressive enrichment of socialist democracy.[10]

An interesting, and instructive, comparison is to look at the practice of the Maoists in Nepal. The Nepali Maoists also realized that the struggle for socialism in the twenty-first century cannot be successful merely through an emulation of the twentieth century struggles. They debated and discussed the question of democracy thoroughly at the Rolpa Plenum, held in May-June 2003, while adopting the document, *The Development of Democracy in the 21st Century*. Nepali Maoist leader Baburam Bhattarai writes:

> After making a critical review of the experiences of revolution and counter-revolution in the 20th century, the document advocated the need to ensure the supervision, intervention and control of the masses over the Party, army and the state in order to

march along the path of continuous revolution after making the revolution, and for this advanced the concept of practicing a multi-party competitive system within the stipulated constitutional framework. This was a new milestone in the development of revolutionary ideas.[11]

On the tenth anniversary of the launching of the peoples' war in Nepal, Maoist leader Prachanda commented in an interview:

One has to be clear about one thing, that our Party is talking about the development of people's democracy in the 21st century after having learnt from the experiences of the revolutions and counter-revolutions of the 20th century, and accordingly has accepted multi-Party competition within an anti-feudal and anti-imperialist constitutional frame.[12]

In spite of the fact that Maoists in Nepal commanded major support through its armed peasant warfare in large parts of the country, they realized that their movement would be unable to go further forward unless they participated in the task of developing a constitutional multi-party democracy replacing the archaic monarchy. In this background the Maoists had entered into a historic agreement with the seven party alliance with other Left and anti-monarchy bourgeois parties. This ensured that they were recognized by the Nepali people as a major force in Nepali politics. Rather than learning from the Nepali Maoists, the Indian Maoists virulently opposed and criticized them and have remained blissfully blind to the question of democracy.

HUMAN RIGHTS VIOLATIONS

Well-meaning liberal intellectuals have been rightly stressing the need for respecting human rights in dealing with the Maoists. But they often seem to overlook the mindless killings that the Maoists indulge in. The liberal opinion legitimately emphasizes that the state should not indulge in fake encounters and other forms of human rights violations. These actions of the state completely undermine the basic principle of natural justice and assumption of innocence until proven guilty, which is the underlying premise of our jurisprudence. Counterproductive campaigns like the Salva Judum in Chhattisgarh, which pit tribals against each other and forces civilians into taking up arms and create anarchy and lawlessness, also need to be opposed. However, none of this absolves the Maoists of their human rights violations. The Maoists' crimes also need to be firmly dealt with as per law.

The Maoists are seldom held accountable by the civil liberties' groups for their heinous actions, particularly the methods that they employ in dealing with their perceived 'class enemies'. These 'class enemies' are often identified in a kangaroo court conducted under the shadow of the gun, usually resulting in a 'death penalty' for ordinary policemen, school teachers, activists of political parties, or other rural poor. The CPI (Maoist) leader Ganapathi has openly defended executions through such kangaroo courts in an article written in the *Economic and Political Weekly* in January 2007:

> In principle, we are against death penalty and our new system that would evolve after the seizure of power will scrap death sentence. But for now the oppressed people and the revolutionaries are compelled to resort to it for their defence; after all, our very survival is at stake if proven counterrevolutionaries are allowed to create havoc with people's lives and pass on information about our movements to the police. As for evidence, let me share with you that recorded cassettes of the entire investigation in the jan adalat, which we had placed by the side of the dead bodies for the world to know, had been taken away by the police.[13]

In other words, while the Maoists are opposed to the death penalty 'in principle' and even promise to 'scrap' the death sentence 'after the seizure of power' when a 'new system' is set up, in the present time they can merrily carry on with assassinations and executions. The rationalization of such brutality against the people is truly confounding. Since the Maoists claim the mantle of being the only true 'revolutionaries', virtually anyone opposed to them is, *ipso facto*, a 'counterrevolutionary'. In insisting that if you are not with the Maoists you are a class enemy, the Maoists mimic the infamous Bush doctrine – either you are with us, or you are with the terrorists! The so-called 'jan adalat' gives no opportunity to the accused to defend him or herself in front of an impartial judge or jury. The Maoist squad leader is, simultaneously, the complainant, prosecutor, judge and executioner, all rolled into one. This is hardly in line with the principles of natural justice or fair trial, and leaving behind a cassette or poster next to the dead body hardly qualifies for evidence. And very often, even this fig leaf of a 'jan adalat' is discarded as too cumbersome, and political opponents are simply assassinated.

Many in the liberal intelligentsia feel concerned, and rightly so, when the state takes recourse to violence against its most poor citizens, often on behalf of the rich and powerful. We must equally realize that the Maoist insistence on violence and 'protracted war' in fact also includes a fair share of human rights violations, which in turn helps legitimize the state's use of armed might. What shrinks, in the end, is the space for democratic dissent and resistance.

CONCLUSION

The struggle against Maoists cannot be carried out successfully merely by banning them or using the strength of security forces. The questions of socio-economic backwardness which dog those very areas where the Maoists operate, have to be urgently addressed and resolved. The grounds of injustice and deprivation in the tribal areas, which are utilized by the Maoists to wage their war against the state, have to be removed.

However, the Maoist response is clearly marked by a stubborn refusal to engage in mass politics and eschew violence, not to speak of giving up arms. Charu Mazumdar – one of the original leaders of the Naxalbari movement who died in police custody, and whom the Maoists continue to deify – had written in his last letter to his wife dated July 14, 1972, that the emphasis on individual assassination in the naxalite movement was a 'deviation'. Charu Mazumdar's warning has fallen on deaf ears. Indian Maoists have stubbornly refused to learn the lessons of history. That is the real tragedy of 'Maoism'.

NOTES

[1] See Chapter 1 of *The Eighteenth Brumaire of Louis Bonaparte*, 1852.

[2] See Chapter 1 of *The Chinese Revolution and the Chinese Communist Party*, 1939.

[3] Ibid.

[4] Chapter 2 of *The Chinese Revolution and the Chinese Communist Party*, 1939.

[5] Ibid.

[6] Section on 'The Struggle for Democracy and Freedom' in *The Tasks of the Chinese Communist Party in the Period of Resistance to Japan*, 1937.

[7] Section on 'Reasons For The Emergence And Survival Of Red Political Power In China' in *Why is it that Red Political Power can Exist in China?*, 1928.

[8] *Comrade Mao Zedong's Historical Role and Mao Zedong Thought*: Resolution on Certain Questions in the History of Our Party Since the Founding of the People's Republic of China (Adopted by the Sixth Plenary session of the Eleventh Central Committee of the Communist Party of China on June 27, 1981).

[9] *Revolutionary Movement in the Colonies and Semi-Colonies*, Sixth Congress of the Communist International, 1928.

[10] See 'Major Shortcomings', *On Certain Ideological Issues* (Resolution Adopted at the 14th Congress of the CPI(M), Madras, January 3–9, 1992).

[11] 'Epochal Ten Years of Application and Development of Revolutionary Ideas', *The Worker*, No. 10, May 2006.

[12] Interview with Prachanda, 'Hoist the Revolutionary Flag in Mount Everest in the 21st Century', *The Worker*, No. 10, May 2006.

[13] See Ganapathi's 'Open Reply to Independent Citizens' Initiative on Dantewada', *Economic and Political Weekly*, January 6, 2007.

The Antinomies of 'Maoism'

Vijay Prashad

In mid-2008, the FARC (Revolutionary Armed Forces of Colombia) came under strong criticism from both Brazil's President Lula and Venezuela's President Chavez. 'The waging of armed struggle as a means of achieving power,' Lula said, 'should end in Latin America. The belief that armed struggle can solve anything is out of date.' Chavez mirrored these views, saying, 'The guerrilla war is history. At this moment in Latin America, an armed guerrilla movement is out of place.' Neither Lula nor Chavez spoke from a position of weakness. Rather, they had been crucial parts of a leftist breakthrough in Latin America, with political forces across South America and into Central America confident enough and respected enough to use the ballot box to attain political power. Former guerrilla organizations, such as the FMLN (El Salvador's Farabundo Marti National Liberation Front), FSLN (Nicaragua's Sandinista National Liberation Front), the MLN (Uruguay's National Liberation Movement, also know as the Tupamaros) and others have all cemented their authority through the electoral process. No more the clandestine meeting, or the gun exchanged in the shadows; now patient organizational work combined with experiments in governance are the order of the day. It is this breakthrough that drew from Lula and Chavez their combined plea for FARC to decommission their troops and enter serious political talks with the Colombian government as a prelude to their entry into the democratic institutions.

Chavez and Lula made a concrete suggestion to FARC. There was no major theoretical move, no issuance of a directive against violence in principle. In 2002, Chavez experienced the strong arm of counter-reaction. It would not be in his experience to underestimate the reaction of the dominant classes and imperialism. They turn to the gun despite their sanctimonious use of the law. Nevertheless, when opportunity presents itself to use the methods of struggle available to expand the reach of the masses into the political institutions, it would be churlish to reject it. In 1902, Lenin was perplexed by the Socialist-Revolutionaries (SR) refusal to come to term with the new mass tempo within Russia, a trend that would lead to the 1905 Revolution. The SR persisted in its policy of political assassinations, with a modest call for mass work (the people, they say, 'alas, are still a long way off'). Then, Lenin let loose:

> We must bear in mind that a revolutionary party is worthy of its name only when it guides *in deed* the movement of a revolutionary class. We must bear in mind that any popular movement assumes an infinite variety of forms, is constantly developing new forms and discarding the old, and effecting modifications or new combinations of old and new forms. It is our duty to participate actively in this process of working out means and methods of struggle. When the students' movement became sharper, we began to call on the workers to come to the aid of the students without taking it upon ourselves to forecast the forms of the demonstrations, without promising that they would result in an immediate transference of strength, in lighting up the mind, or a special elusiveness. When the demonstrations became consolidated, we began to call for their organization and for the arming of the masses, and put forward the task of preparing a popular uprising. Without in the least denying violence and terrorism in principle, we demanded work for the preparation of such forms of violence as were calculated to bring about the direct participation of the masses and which guaranteed that participation. We do not close our eyes to the difficulties of this task, but will work at it steadfastly and persistently, undeterred by the objections that this is a matter of the 'vague and distant future.' Yes, gentlemen, we stand for future and not only past forms of the movement. We give preference to long and arduous work on what promises a future rather than to an 'easy' repetition of what has been condemned by the past. We shall always expose people who in word war against hackneyed dogmas and in practice hold exclusively to such moth-eaten and harmful commonplaces as the theory of the transference of strength, the difference between big work and petty work and, of course, the theory of single combat.[1]

Terrorism of the SR variety, and to transpose the matter, of the Maoist kind, has, Lenin continued, 'the immediate effect of simply creating a short-lived sensation while indirectly it even leads to apathy and passive waiting for the next *bout.*' The more effective an act of terror, the more it sends the masses back home, waiting for a great avenger to take action on their behalf. A movement that is driven by terror and violence might excite interest in the short term, but since it does not change the structure of exploitation, and since the old systems come back into play once more, the excitement leads to disillusionment. The main barometer to judge a political action, as Lenin points out, is not whether it is violent or not, but whether it is 'calculated to bring about direct participation of the masses and guarantee their participation.' That is the *ne plus ultra* of political action. It is why a large section of the SR joined the Bolsheviks in late 1917.

VENEZUELA

Chavez is no stranger to the armed road. His brother Adan, now a leading Chavista, was a member of the Revolutionary Left Movement (MIR), a Marxist-Leninist guerrilla organization, and later with the Party of the Venezuelan Revolution, an urban underground organization affiliated with the former guerrilla commander Douglas Bravo. From Adan, Hugo Chavez also saw first hand the limitations of this work. As Adan put it to Alan Woods, 'We conducted urban guerrilla work. But because of [the] clandestine character [of the Party of the Venezuelan Revolution, it] did not have contact with the masses. Furthermore they were very dogmatic and sectarian. Like the MIR, it split and ended up disappearing. In order to achieve a revolutionary popular movement, which would allow the taking of power, one had to have a strong influence within the popular masses and have support within the Armed Forces.'[2] Adan's prognosis mirrors the self-criticism of the Venezuelan Armed Forces of National Liberation (FALN), whose leadership wrote in 1964 that they had fallen prey to 'infantile subjectivism of petty bourgeois origin – the swollen enthusiasm due to a long chain of successes which we gained for a time, which made us appear each day, in Venezuela as well as abroad, like an almost mythological force of immeasurable power.'[3] This led to an underestimation of the Venezuelan state and a grave overestimation of the fellowship between the masses and the FALN. The assessment is gloomy, but its victim was not simply the guerrilla army. It was equally the Venezuelan Communist Party, which took refuge in small acts that did not challenge the Venezuelan oligarchy. It was its timidity that led to its open break with Castro's Cuba in 1967 (made spectacular by Castro's speech at the August meeting of the First Latin American Conference of

Solidarity[4]).

Hugo Chavez was part of the Venezuelan armed forces, within which he led a small clandestine leftist group.[5] His band attempted a coup in 1992 that failed. Hugo Chavez went on television to tell his comrades to give up, *por ahora* (for now). That phrase, *por ahora*, struck a chord. Chavez converted his popularity into a mass movement, into which the small parties and the social movements threw themselves. I remember meeting various left activists at the Central University of Venezuela in the years between the Chavez coup attempt (1992) and before his eventual electoral victory (1998) – their gloom was evident, nostalgia for Cuba, circa 1959, but desolation for their own future. Guerrilla warfare had ended by the mid-1990s: the leading edge for the Maoists of the continent was the Shining Path of Peru, whose leader, Abimael Guzman, was captured by the Peruvian military in 1991, with mopping up operations at work around the Maoists' stronghold of Ayacucho. The Venezuelan left activists were in small bands, unable yet to see what had begun in the barrios, the slums of the poor that ring the city.

The fatigue with the parties of the Right and the Center-Right and the enthusiasm for the populism of Chavez' party and his style enabled the first victory. Against US pressure and the machinations of the oligarchy, Chavez's movement held firm. It then conducted its 'long march through the institutions,' bringing the various state agencies in line with the values of the Bolivarian movement. All this culminated in the revision of the Constitution, which now better represented the aspirations of the vast mass of the Venezuelan population. State power was the goal, but it had been clear to the Bolivarian movement that state power does not only mean control of the state apparatus; if it meant only this, then the Bolivarians would have to do the dirty work of the oligarchy's 1961 Constitution.

To write the new Bolivarian Constitution (1999), the Venezuelan population voted in a Constituent Assembly, who drafted a Constitution, which was then ratified in a popular vote, the first time ever in the country's history. The Constitution draws from a variety of sources, including from Latin America's revolutionary history (from the liberator Simon Bolivar and the Marxist Jose Carlos Mariategui) and from Marxist theory (notably the remarkable Soviet jurist Evgeny Pashukanis). It is an astounding document, with provisions for deeper democracy at one level, and another for the widest recognition of human rights. The Chavez government had already formed the *Barrio Adentro* programme to provide government-sponsored healthcare for the population. But this would have simply been at the mercy of the government. Now, the Constitution directs the government to provide healthcare, as it is legally binding. All of this funded, propitiously, by the oil revenues that flooded into Venezuela's state coffers. Guns remained holstered. The struggle was taken through the ballot box.[6]

The successes of the Bolivarian project threatened the oligarchy with extinction and the US with the loss of its own power in its backyard. Distracted by the wars in Afghanistan and Iraq, as well as by the nuclear ambitions of North Korea and Iran, the US was unable to extend itself against the Bolivarians. The armies in the region too were not enthused to leave the barracks. The tide of history in Latin America favoured the Bolivarians. Nevertheless, the US pushed for a counter-revolutionary coup in 2002. It failed, as the people rallied in large numbers behind the Bolivarian project. They had everything to lose, and they had been organized for just this eventuality. Chavez would not allow himself to fall like Chile's Salvador Allende (whose regime was overthrown in a CIA-inspired military coup in 1973). Chavez had the support of the military, and he had not allowed the population to remain demobilized. They were now part of neighborhood committees and various self-defence leagues. They won by the numbers. The time of 'terrible necessity,' to unholster the gun, was not yet at hand.

BRAZIL

Lula, too, was also no stranger to the politics of the gun. When he was nineteen, the military deposed the left-liberal President Joåo Goulart to open an era of military rule that ran from 1964 to 1985. Lula lost the little finger of his left hand while working a press in an auto factory during the coup year, and by the time the dictatorship ended, he was a leader in the trade union movement and in the Workers' Party (PT). During this long era, the urban middle class that leaned left went either into the clandestine trade union organizational work or into the clandestine urban guerrilla units. Of the latter, the most spectacular was Carlos Marighella's National Liberation Alliance; Marighella was the author of the influential *Mini Manual of the Urban Guerrilla* (June 1969), a touchstone for the urban guerrilla from Montevideo to Mexico City. The police killed Marighella the same year as his manual came out (he was 57 years old, a veteran of the Brazilian CP who had broken with it over the strategy of violence).

The urban guerrilla did not influence Lula. Nor did the sectarianism of the Brazilian Communist Party during the Goulart era. The Brazilian CP took a hard line against the left-liberal regime of Goulart, letting him feel the heat from both the much less powerful Left and the much more powerful Right-wing (principally the oligarchy and the military). In 1965, the Central Committee of the Brazilian CP conceded its errors, mainly 'the underestimation of the danger of a rightist coup, which was considered to be a mere scarecrow, intended to frighten the masses. Concentrating our fire on the government, we demanded more and more drastic measures while overlooking our own weaknesses and the shortcomings of the national-democratic movement, as well as the effective correlation of social forces that existed at that time.'[7]

The lessons for Lula were straightforward, and these went with him and the other labour activists into the Workers' Party (PT) in 1980. A few years later, the Brazilian campesinos formed two of the most resilient peasant organizations, the National Confederation of Agricultural Workers and Movimiento Los Sin Tierra (MST) – they built up a membership of about eleven million members. These groups became fundamental constituents of the PT, and began to work with the burgeoning Communist Party of Brazil (which had by the late 1970s recovered significant ground). Even in the most difficult situation, Lula and his current remained with mass organizing, building a movement of Brazilian workers through small actions that enhanced the confidence of individuals to create a strong collectivity. It was this long campaign that resulted in the *Diretas Ja!* (Direct Elections Now) movement of 1984 that finally toppled the dictatorship. Not once did Lula move to the gun. Some of this is certainly temperamental; he was a working-class organizer who believed in making the fullest use of whatever institutions are available to build the power of the working-class.[8]

CUBA

It was not easy for a Latin American leftist to stray too far from the gun. US imperialism has always treated Latin America as its property. The Roosevelt Corollary (1904) to the Monroe Doctrine (1823) pointed out that the US government had the right to intervene in Latin America when it saw instances of 'flagrant and chronic wrongdoing by a Latin American Nation'. It was for the US President to make this assessment. And he made it often, from the 1846 invasion of Mexico to the 2009 soft coup in Honduras. If the US did not come by way of the Marines or the Bombers, it came equally powerfully with its Dollars and Free Trade Agreements. This was clear to the Uruguayan Communist Party leader Rodney Arismendi by 1947, when he wrote, 'The United States is profiting from this vying for power, from advantages obtained during the war, and in particular from commitments and agreements made under the Pan-American system. There is, therefore, no Pan American economic combination that does not lay South America at the feet of Yankee industry.' A combined Latin America needed to stand tall against the attempt by 'Anglo-Yankee financial oligarchies', which were trying to 'dynamite the foundation of the newly laid peace'.[9] Any attempt to push a peace agenda was met with the same tonic from the local oligarchs and their North American allies: military coups and murder of the organizers of the peace. No wonder the gun for the revolutionary.

The agony of the Left saw its deliverance in 1959 with the Cuban Revolution. It was almost miraculous. A small detachment of poorly armed men and women came off a boat from Mexico to hold off the Cuban military in the highlands. From there, luck and pluck enabled them to enlarge their base (their *foco*) and create firm alliances with the urban mass movements, which had themselves been awoken from a deep slumber by Castro and his brigands. The dictatorship crumbled with a few armed engagements. It was an extraordinary moment. Young people across Latin America took refuge in it, and, in particular, with Che Guevara's call to revolt (his *Guerrilla Warfare*, 1961). The French student, Regis Debray, wrote a manifesto for Castroism (1965), which extolled the ideas in motion, which do not exist 'except in those towns and mountains where at the present moment thousands of militants are fighting, beleaguered, with no guarantee for the future.' Debray was careful to point out in his survey that the tendency had already failed to take flight ('armed struggle is not in itself a panacea'), and yet he willed the idea of the 'organic link between armed struggle and mass struggle.'[10] Debray's teacher, Louis Althusser responded tartly, 'It may be that your theses are correct, but your text doesn't really provide a positive demonstration of this; it simply gives what we could call a negative demonstration. In your writings, the validity of guerrilla warfare is demonstrated less by its own merits than through the defects or drawbacks of past forms of struggle that you examine; it is supported less by its positive qualities than by the negative aspects of other forms of struggle.'[11]

Che Guevara decamped to Bolivia, to try out his method for the last time. He went to a remote region, hoping to enthuse the peasantry of the north-east and the miners to throw in their lot with him against the military dictatorship of René Barrientos. Che was isolated. Even the army's massacre at San Juan (70 dead) did not prevent the miners, the most radical section of the working-class, from cutting a deal with the government for better conditions and wages. Che felt betrayed. The 'necessary minimum' that he had sketched out in his *Guerrilla Warfare* had not been attained: the people did not 'see clearly the futility of maintaining the fight for social goals within the framework of civil debate.' For the Bolivians, peace was not 'considered already broken.'[12] Only if the people *saw* that civil debate was no longer possible, and that war had already broken out, then 'popular discontent expresses itself in more active forms. An attitude of resistance finally crystallizes in an outbreak of fighting, provoked initially by the conduct of the authorities.'

Che's band could not swim like fish in the sea, but it was too late. The futility of the effort comes across in Che's last entry into his diary: 'Eleven months since our inauguration as guerrillas; the day was being spent without complications, even bucolically, until 12:30 when an old woman shepherding her goats came into the canyon where we had camped and it was necessary to apprehend her. The woman gave no truthful news about the soldiers, saying that she didn't know anything, as it was a long time since she had been here. She only gave information about the roads. . . . Fifty pesos were given to her with the request that she not say a word, but with little hope that she would keep her promise.'[13] Not only were the guerrillas isolated geographically, but also they were isolated from the people. They did not trust them. It is this image that provoked Teodoro Petkoff of the Venezuelan CP and then of the MAS (Movimiento al Socialismo), and now a fierce critic of Chavez, to write in 1976, 'Reality showed that a revolutionary will, deprived of favourable circumstances and supported by generalities like "Latin America is ready for revolution" could do nothing when faced with those "stony eyes" of the Bolivian peasants who looked at Guevara without understanding his efforts to communicate with them.'[14]

By 1976, when Petkoff wrote his screed, the guerrilla movements had percolated into driblets. Little remained in the Southern Cone (Argentina, Uruguay, Chile), and much less still in Brazil and Venezuela. Bolivia had been rendered mute, and Paraguay never was much of an option. The activists who remained alive took refuge in incubation: they seeded movements with their careful gestures, working among the Amerindians or the trade unions, in the very densest Amazon forests or in the densest working-class barrios. The armed struggle, however, took root in the Andes, from southern Peru to the highlands of Colombia. In the former, it was the Shining Path, which would be obliterated by the mid-1990s. In the latter, it was the FARC.

PERU

Cuba's 'revolutionary audacity' sent a tremor through Latin America. In Peru, it appealed to the students, many of whom bristled to live in a society where 0.1 per cent of the population, in 1964, owned over 60 per cent of the land. These landlords exercised their power without any of the liberal niceties set in place by the Constitution of 1933. The province of Ayacucho was Peru's second poorest, with a per capita income less than a third of the national average. One remarkable feature of Peru's history was the creation of educational institutions across the country, and in this case, the re-opening of the Huamanga University in 1959 in impoverished Ayacucho. Radical students found themselves in a rural outpost, with high levels of feudal injustice meted out by landlords in collusion with the state against Amerindians. Carlos Ivan Degregori called this situation 'a veritable social earthquake'.[15]

A professor of philosophy, Abimael Guzmán, began to teach at the university, in what would become a 'temple to Mao Zedong'. A group formed around Guzmán, Peruvian Communist Party members largely and students, who met in his house, jokingly called El Kremlin. In 1969, Guzmán's faction broke from the Communist Party to found the Partido Comunista del Perú-Sendero Luminoso, the Shining Path.[16] They threatened armed struggle, but contented themselves to building up their bases in the university and in the countryside. These fifteen years of relative quiet came during the 'military-socialist' regime of General Juan Velasco Alvardo (1968–1975), which was not only pro-Beijing but also attempted to produce some elements of social reform (nationalization, agrarian reform, and so on). '*Campesino, el dueño nunca mas va a comer de tu pobreza,*' said Velasco Alvardo: 'Peasant, the landlord will no longer eat from your poverty.' 360,000 families took possession of many of the highland haciendas. The tendency toward reform had set into Peruvian society. A new Constitution was adopted in 1979 that gave the military a far less central role in Peruvian affairs. Even severe economic crises in the late 1970s could not fully derail the reform dynamic. As democracy began to settle in, Sendero announced that it had begun its armed struggle.[17]

'Elections have never given the working class or the people power,' Guzmán declared in 1980, 'and it can only be conquered through prolonged and hard armed struggle. The state's foundation has fractured. The substantive problems ailing the country have to do with this. The crisis derives from there.'[18] Guzmán believed that any participation in the elections would strengthen the state. The point of the Maoist insurgency was to destroy the state. It was this rigid position against any 'collaboration' with the state that began Sendero's path to mass killings. Early attacks on drug dealers and thieves as well as landlords were appreciated by the down-trodden peasantry. But the killings did not stop there. Sendero went after anyone whom it considered to be collaborating with the state. School teachers who were respected in their localities were killed; particularly those who refused to introduce Maoism of the Guzmán variety (what is known as Gonzalo Thought) into the classroom. Sendero went after the model agricultural societies set up as part of the agrarian reform. As well, the partisans assassinated priests and nuns and anyone who was associated with the provision of social relief (they were seen as 'shock absorbers of the regime,' institutions that 'dampened revolutionary consciousness'). The 'class enemy' was not the dominant class, interestingly, but the members of the leftist bloc, Izquierda Unida which grew out of the Revolutionary Left Movement, a group founded by Luis de la Puente Uceda in 1962, inspired by the Cuban Revolution. By 1980, the best organizers of the Movement formed the above ground IU. In 1992, Sendero killed the legendary Lima-based organizer, Maria Elena Moyano, an Afro-Peruvian woman who was a leader of the shantytowns. They killed her because they wanted to muscle into her neighborhood of Villa El Salvador, and needed her out of the way.[19]

In April 1983, Sendero killed eighty people, including a six-month old child, in the town of Lucanamarca. Guzmán justified this massacre:

> ... more than 80 were annihilated, this is the reality, and we say
> it, here there was excess. But our problem was to give a bruising
> blow to restrain them, to make them understand that the thing was
> not so easy. I reiterate, the principle thing was to make them
> understand that we were a hard bone to chew, and that we were
> ready to do anything, anything.[20]

Ideas, Guzmán felt, needed to be 'pounded into [the peasantry's]
heads with dramatic deeds.' The 'fistful' of Sendero partisans would
lead the people 'across a river of blood.' Guzmán liked to channel Mao,
that: 'violence is a universal law and without revolutionary violence
one class cannot be substituted for another, an old order cannot be
overthrown to create a new one.' Violence was not part of a larger
strategy. It was part of Sendero's aesthetic: 'the people's blood has a rich
perfume,' went the Sendero song, *Flor de Retama*, 'like jasmine, daisies,
geraniums and violets.' 'Blood will not drown the revolution, but water
it,' chanted the Sendero cadre as they entered villages, guns with the
safety off. Violence was tactic, strategy and goal. It was everything.

Peru's Commission on Truth and Reconciliation reported that
between 1980 and 2000, 69,280 had been killed during what is called,
in Quechua, *chaqwa*, the trauma, the chaos (the other phrase is *manchay
tiempo*, time of fear). Hundreds of thousands of people fled their homes
for Lima and other cities, now overly congested. By the Commission's
analysis Sendero was responsible for 54 per cent of the deaths, while the
counterinsurgency of the brutal military killed 31 per cent. The rest fell
at the hands of peasants who organized themselves against Sendero into
rondas campesinas (peasants who make the rounds). If the *rondas* decided
to fight fire with fire, in 1988 a section of women formed the *Federación
Provincial de Clubes de Madres de Huamanga* to hold a rally against the
violence. 'Because we give life we defend it,' they chanted, and 'the fear
is gone.' The Sendero guerrillas tried to disrupt the rally, but, as one
scholar put it, the women fought back, 'I have never seen such strength,
decision and fury, as when those women leaders went up to the dais and
screamed and hit the intruders until they had to recede.' Such popular
revulsion, combined with the arrest of Guzmán and the Central
Committee in 1991, stunted Sendero's line of march. It has now

dissolved into small bands, sustained by coca trafficking and the occasional ambush of police forces.

COLOMBIA

The armed struggle in Peru is now a sideshow, a cottage industry. A few attacks here and there disrupt everyday life every so often. Nothing more. This is not the case in Colombia, where the FARC remains a powerful force in large sections of the country. But it has come to a stalemate, which is why Chavez and Lula have called upon the FARC to revisit its strategy.

Formed in 1964 by a rump group of the Colombian Communist Party (and led by the remarkable leader Manuel Marulanda, also known as Tiro Fijo, 'sure shot'), the FARC went deep into the roots of Colombia's rural life (*Colombia profunda*), building rural leadership to replace the few urban militants who had retreated into the countryside. Massive assault by the US-financed Colombian military could not destroy it, and indeed it seemed to grow like a mythical beast with each attack. In the 1980s, the Colombian Left signed a peace agreement with the oligarchy, and took to the polls. FARC created an above-ground electoral instrument, the Unión Patriótica (UP). A similar dynamic opened up in Ireland at around this time, when the Sinn Féin, as the electoral arm of the IRA, began to cease its policy of abstaining from the political domain. The UP won some small victories, but largely failed to make a break into national politics. Nevertheless, a space had opened up in the 1980s to bring the FARC's considerable strength to bear on national policy. It was not to be. The right-wing paramilitary groups, with the collusion of the military, began to assassinate the UP members, even after the UP broke with the FARC. By 2002, the UP vanished. Its demise gives the FARC even less incentive to experiment with the enervated democratic institutions. Through the UP period, FARC retained its guns, it did not leave the country for the cities. There was no Bolivarian project in the 1980s, nor was US imperialism distracted by the Middle East. Nor indeed was there a viable left-liberal electoral formation outside the FARC. FARC restarted the armed struggle. It was the resilience of the FARC that pushed the Plan Colombia, with the US government making that country the base of its Latin American operations. But it could not defeat FARC. The situation went to a stalemate.[21]

It is in this stalemate that other forces emerged. In the northern regions, where the FARC is also popular, came new social institutions of the Nasa Indians. They held peace in their hearts, exhausted by the protracted civil war that has claimed too many of their loved ones. For them, another path was necessary. FARC was not going anywhere. It bounced back from its demise in 1970–74, and neither Plan Colombia (1998–2006) nor Plan Patriota (2003–2006) has dented the stalemate. And yet, as Colombian activist and economist Hector Mondragon put it recently, the FARC has long eschewed the mass line for the military line. It is devoted to its military campaign, and pays little attention to the building up of mass struggles. As Mondragon points out, 'This is a political error. It has become a tragedy for popular struggles. It has permitted the strengthening of the extreme right, which today is running the country. Not only has it failed to stop the displacement of hundreds of thousands of peasants and afro-Colombians, but it has actually exacerbated that process, and even provoked the forced displacement of indigenous peoples in various parts of the country.'[22] From this perspective one must see Chavez and Lula's plea to FARC. They want the muscle of this organization to come above ground, join the leftwing wave in Latin America by assisting the Democratic Pole and other left-liberal formations move Colombia's institutions leftward.

PHILIPPINES

This is a pattern that is replicated across the Pacific Ocean, in the Maoist Communist Party of the Philippines (CPP). Formed in 1968, the CPP hastened to make linkages with the scattered elements of the guerrillas that had survived the crackdown against the Huk Rebellion (1946–1954). Inspired by the Cultural Revolution in China and by Mao in particular, the CPP settled itself into the countryside. In the midst of his second term as President, Ferdinand Marcos abolished the rule of law and governed by Martial Law (1972–1981). 'As a matter of principle' the CPP did not join fully with the anti-Marcos movement, and missed the immense opportunity given to the people by the wave that eventually swept Marcos from Martial Law and then, in 1986, from office. The CPP grudgingly worked in united front organizations, even being a part of BAYAN (New Patriotic Alliance). But at each turn, the itch for the 'people's war' kicked in. Later, CPP leader Jose Maria Sisson recognized that left sectarianism contributed to the call for an 'active boycott' of the elections. In 1985–86, no such self-reflection was on offer. As the people's movements clamored for the democratic institutions, the CPP chased the gun.

The CPP in the Philippines, like the Shining Path in Peru, underestimated the ideological impact of the restoration of the democratic process. Under massive political pressure, Marcos withdrew in 1986. The field lay open for creative united front tactics. But the CPP went on its own. The pull of the democratic process drew many cadres. They did not grasp the need for violence and the armed struggle. The protracted war did not make sense in the context of the democratic opening. Reckless politics led to the death or defection of half of the CPP's cadre. In 1993, the CPP went on the hunt against 'revisionism', afraid of further loss of members to the parliamentary road. The way forward was to conduct what it called 'death condemnations', to sentence members to death as a way to chill dissent within the CPP. In 1994, the CPP assassinated one of its former leaders, Leopoldo 'Ka Hector' Mabilangan, who had taken advantage of a government amnesty to come overground the previous year. Jose Maria Sisson, the CPP chief, defended this assassination to a comrade, who wrote about it a decade later:

> When I asked for the reason for this killing, [Sisson] replied that it was necessary to 'kill the chicken to scare the monkey'. I didn't understand what this meant at first, but later I found out that this was one of the tactics used by Mao during his various inner party struggles – kill a lower official as a warning to the higher official that he was fighting against. Ka Hector's death was a warning to others.[23]

The death condemnations continue, with activist and intellectual Walden Bello being in its sights (the CPP denies it now). Bello is a deputy in the Congress of the Philippines' House of Representatives as the second nominee of the leftwing Akbayan party. The various left formations, including the PMP-Merger and Akbayan do not characterize the nature of the Filipino state as 'semi-colonial, semi-feudal'. Rather, they see it as a form of underdeveloped capitalism, where a variety of struggles (mass and parliamentary struggles, including, if the balance of forces calls for it, military struggle) are necessary to transform the system. The frisson of the Bolivarian breakthrough is evident in these circles, most of whom have taken their lessons from the anti-dictatorship movement of the 1980s and the transformation in Filipino capitalism over the past twenty years. The state is not so weak that a few gunshots can bring it to its knees, and nor yet is the state's ideological apparatuses so worthless that the people have no fealty to the state's institutions or to the siren of capitalist consumerism.

MASS NOT GUNS

The question of the 'armed road' requires a thoughtful consideration of the terrain of power, and of the political economy of contemporary capitalism in less developed societies. What is the role of the domestic dominant class, and what is its relationship with imperialism? If it is simply an offshoot of imperialism with no depth into the fabric of society, then a small nudge will dispatch it. If, on the other hand, capitalist relations are reasonably developed, the ideological state apparatus is robust and the domestic dominant class has a strategic relationship with imperialism rather than merely being a 'comprador', then matters are much more complex. For any Communist party, at the bare minimum, one must have a discussion on these issues, at least hold some kind of conclave or conference, the desideratum of democratic political life.

The CPP in the Philippines has only held one party congress (in 1968), as did the Shining Path (in 1988). There have been few democratic spaces, even within these parties, to discuss the structures and conjunctures within which the Left must act. This demonstrates contempt for the experience of the members of the Party, whose own work shows a reconsideration of the strategy (and hence has led to either defection or assassinations). Che's 'necessary minimum' does not operate when the armed road has become a religion. Che remarks, in *Guerrilla Warfare*, 'Where a government has come into power through some form of popular vote, fraudulent or not, and maintains at least an appearance of constitutional legality, the guerrilla outbreak cannot be promoted, since the possibilities of peaceful struggle have not yet been exhausted'. Che's 'necessary minimum' reflects the thinking of the Third International's Third Congress:

Action must be prepared and organized in such a way that the broadest masses recognize the struggle as one for their own most pressing needs and therefore rally to the movement. The more precarious the position of world capital, the harder will the capitalists try to smash any vanguard which loses contact with the broad masses and to frustrate the future victory of the Communist International. This danger can be averted if the Communist Parties initiate a mass agitational campaign that reaches and rouses all sections of the working people; if they engage in energetic organizational work that strengthens the Party's influence on the broad masses and makes possible a sober evaluation of the field of struggle; and if they adopt the tactic of retreating when the enemy has superior forces and attacking when the enemy forces are scattered and the masses united.

Such an assessment had to be careful not to underestimate the use of violence by the power bloc from above. In 1973, Communist Party of India (Marxist) leader E.M.S. Namboodiripad spoke in an important seminar in Kolkata on 'Chile and the Parliamentary Road to Socialism.' EMS carefully delineated the differences between the Chilean example and the Indian one. In Chile the various Left parties had come together to form the Popular Unity coalition (UP in its Spanish initials) that had gained popular support and eventually, through elections, the presidency. However, the UP did not control the parliament, nor did it constrain the power of the oligarchs. The Chilean Left could take as much comfort in the views of Chile's oligarchy as the Indian Left could in the Indian bourgeoisie. A counter-revolution would come, and the question, EMS raised, was how could it be defeated. The Chilean Left's weakness over the military 'could have been overcome if the government of the Popular Unity bloc had used its power to arm the people, or a split had taken place within the armed forces.'[24] From this analysis, EMS surmised that the parliamentary road remained the necessary one for the Left, and yet, once in power, the Left should never assume that it would be allowed to rule based on the protections of the Constitution. The reactionaries will come in the dark of night, armed and ready to do mayhem. It is for this inevitability that the Left must prepare. The way the Venezuelan people thwarted the 2002 coup attempt follows EMS in all its particulars.

It is commonplace for Peruvian organizers of the Left to speak about being trapped between 'two fires', that of the Peruvian state and of Sendoro (Shining Path). The guns fired from both ends, killed their militants and smothered the space to build their movements. A few years ago, the General Secretary of the Peruvian Communist Party, Renán Raffo Muñoz, told a journalist that there is as yet no political movement that has transformed the 'political and social discontent of the people'. When it comes to the elections, the people remain wedded to the Right. This is because the Left is not well organized, and 'because we were not able to create sound political programmes and projects. . . . Our people are looking for concrete gestures. Many of them don't care about ideology.'[25] The General Confederation of Peruvian Workers, the Communist Party and the various small left political formations now struggle to expand their base, to find a new praxis on the terrain of mass politics.

Much the same dynamic is at work in the Philippines, where, in 2005, the major Left sections (minus the CPP) formed the Laban ng Masa (Struggle of the Masses) as a platform for the mobilization of the people. Then again, in 2009, various social movement organizations formed the Partido Lakas ng Masa (Power of the Masses Party), a socialist formation, whose chairperson Sonny Melencio noted, 'The socialist victories in Latin America were not simply victories in the ballot boxes. Those electoral victories were preceded by popular uprisings that mobilized millions of people. During the elections, these uprisings were transformed into giant mobilizations but the mobilizations are also continuing in an ongoing process of building new institutions of popular power.'[26]

Mass politics is the key for all these parties that are operating to find a new social base of the oppressed and exploited. They come from many places, some from experience with the gun and others from the various social movements. But the lesson is the same: the time of the armed struggle is, as Chavez put it, 'out of place' when mass confidence has to be built, and it is 'out of place,' as well, where a Leftist breakthrough has occurred. The gun retreats to the closet.

NOTES

[1] Lenin, *Revolutionary Adventurism, Iskra*, No. 23, August 1, and No. 24, September 1, 1902.

[2] 'A Conversation of Alan Woods with Adan Chavez,' *In Defense of Marxism*, April 18, 2005.

[3] FALN, 'Our Errors,' *Studies on the Left*, IV, November 4 ,1964.

[4] Fidel Castro, 'Speech to the OLAS Conference,' August 10, 1967. Available on-line at http://www.marxists.org/history/cuba/archive/castro/1967/08/10.htm.

[5] For more on Chavez, see Nikolas Kozloff, *Hugo Chavez: Oil, Politics and the Challenge to the U. S.*, New York: Palgrave, 2007 and for more on the Bolivarian Revolution, see Gregory Wilpert, *Changing Venezuela by Taking Power: The History and Policies of the Chavez Government*, London: Verso, 2006.

[6] For more on the social condition of the Bolivarian Revolution, and its base, see Sujatha Fernandes, *Who Can Stop the Drums? Urban Social Movements in Chavez's Venezuela*, Durham: Duke University Press, 2010.

[7] 'La situación en Brasil,' *Principios*, no. 108, Santiago, August 1965.

[8] For a reasonable analysis of Lula's tenure and politics, see Emir Sader, 'Brazil Takes Lula's Measure,' *Dispatches from Latin America. Experiments Against Neoliberalism*, Eds. Teo Ballvé and Vijay Prashad, New Delhi: Leftword, 2006.

[9] Rodney Arismendi, 'El Fín de la Guerra y el Nuevo imperialismo norteamericano,' *Para un prontuario del dolar (al margen del Plan Truman)*, Montevideo: Ediciones Pueblos Unidos, 1947.

[10] Regis Debray, 'Latin America: The Long March,' *New Left Review*, I/33, September-October 1965.

[11] Quoted in Regis Debray, *La Critique des Armes*, Paris: Seuil, 1974.

[12] Che Guevara, *Guerrilla Warfare*, New York: Monthly Review Press, 1961.

[13] Che Guevara, *The Bolivian Diary*, Melbourne: Ocean Press, 2006.

[14] Teodoro Petkoff, *Proceso a la Izquierda, o de la Falsa Conducta Revolucionaria*, Caracas: Editorial Planeta, 1976.

[15] Carlos Ivan Degregori, *Ayacucho 1969-1979: El surgimiento de Sendero Luminoso*, Lima: Insituto de Estudioso Peruanos, 1990. Degregori was on the Peruvian Truth and Reconciliation Commission.

[16] For a good introduction to Sendero, see *Shining and other Paths: War and Society in Peru, 1980-1995*, ed. Steve Stern, Durham: Duke University Press, 1998.

[17] For the pre-history of Sendero, see Grant Hilliker, *The Politics of Reform in Peru*, Baltimore: Johns Hopkins University Press, 1971 and James Petras, Morris Morley and A. Eugene Havens, 'Peru: Capitalist Democracy in Transition,' *New Left Review*, I/142, November-December 1983.

[18] Gustavo Gorriti, *Shining Path. A History of the Millenarian War in Peru*, Chapel Hill: University of North Carolina Press, 1997.

[19] See, Maria Elena Moyano, *The Autobiography of Maria Elena Moyano: the Life and Death of a Peruvian Activist*, University Press of Florida, 2000.

[20] Quoted by Carlos Ivan Degregori, 'Harvesting Storms: Peasant *Rondas* and the Defeat of Sendero Luminoso in Ayachucho,' *Shining and other paths*.

[21] Forrest Hylton, *Evil Hour in Colombia*, London: Verso, 2006.

[22] Hector Mondragon, 'On my choice of Civil Resistance,' *ZNET*, September 10, 2008.

[23] There are number of interviews with Sison where he makes these assertions. For instance, David Glanz, *The Implosion of the Communist Party of the Philippines: An interview with Jose Maria Sison*, Monash University Working Papers no. 92, 1995 and *Jose Maria Sison: At Home in the World – Portrait of a Revolutionary*, in conversation with Ninotchka Rosca, Greensboro, NC: Open Hand, 2004. The quote above comes from the CPP's Carlo Butalid, in an interview with Pierre Rousset, February 16, 2003.

[24] E. M. S. Namboodiripad, 'Chile and the Parliamentary Road to Socialism,' *Social Scientist*, Vol. 2, No. 5, Dec. 1973.

[25] Andre Vltchek, 'The Left in Peru,' *ZNET*, August 8, 2002.

[26] Sonny Melencio at the foundation of the Partido Lakas ng Masa of the Philippines, January 30, 2009.

Appendix

Ideological Debate Summed Up
[Excerpts]
Polit Bureau, Communist Party of India (Marxist)
June, 1968

Let us take up the main points of their (left-sectarian) criticism levelled against our Party Programme.

They challenge the correctness of our characterization of Indian independence as 'political independence', and call it 'formal independence' or 'nominal independence'.

They challenge the class character of the present Indian state and government as made in our Party Programme – a bourgeois-landlord state led by the big bourgeoisie which is collaborating with foreign capital in pursuance of their capitalist path of development – and assert that it is a 'neo-colonial state with a puppet regime serving mainly the imperialists and feudalists.' They, in order to buttress the above two points of theirs, characterize the present Indian big industrial bourgeoisie as comprador bourgeoisie, which acts as the 'lackey', 'puppet' and 'stooge' of U.S. imperialism.

They emphasize exclusively the collaboration aspect of the Indian big bourgeoisie with foreign monopoly capital and refuse to take note of the conflicts and contradictions that do exist between them.

They assess the internal and external policies of the present Indian state and government from the above stated standpoint of theirs and tend to negate the extent of the capitalist development that has taken place in the industrial and agricultural sectors during the last two decades, and depict it as merely strengthening of foreign imperialism, native feudalism and the Indian big comprador class.

All these differences with the Party Programme to a superficial observer may appear to be minor or matters of greater or lesser emphasis on certain aspects. But a careful analysis reveals that they are of a vital and fundamental nature. If all these are accepted as correct, the Party

Programme cannot have any legs to stand on and will cease to be valid anymore. It can remain and serve the Party only if these are rejected as totally wrong and utterly untenable.

Such is the essence of the problem before us.

CONCEPT OF FORMAL INDEPENDENCE AND WHAT IT IMPLIES

Is this controversy, that of 'formal independence' versus 'political independence', new in our Party?

No. It was there for a long time. The Second Party Congress in its *Political Thesis* characterized the newly won independence as formal independence; the 1951 Party Programme again had characterized the 'independence' as formal. This position of ours was maintained doggedly till the year 1954–55. Several Communist leaders in the international communist movement subscribed to the very same view and were analysing Indian developments following the transfer of political power and British withdrawal, from the same standpoint. This position was sought to be defended by a passage from Lenin's theses 'On the National and Colonial Question' adopted at the Second Congress of the C.I. which reads: 'The need constantly to explain and expose among the broadest working masses of all countries, and particularly of the backward countries, the deception systematically practised by the imperialist powers, which under the guise of politically independent states, set up states that are wholly dependent upon them economically, financially and militarily'.

Then, where does the mistake lie?

It lies in the fact that this absolutely correct statement of Lenin about the deceptive tricks of imperialist powers to set up formally independent regimes 'under the guise of politically independent states' is sought to be applied mechanically to the post-second world war situation when world imperialism has been very much weakened, when there has been a radical shift in the correlation of forces in the international arena against imperialism, and when the capacity of various imperialist powers to practise their old deception and trickery against the colonial and dependent peoples is severely curtailed. Failure to assess these big developments correctly in the world arena has led many to put a lop-sided emphasis on one aspect, namely, the deception practised by the imperialist powers and consequently underestimate the growing strength of and the new possibilities for the world anti-imperialist forces to fight the imperialist deception, to win and defend political independence and to struggle for economic independence.

It was this mistake that led our Party in the period 1948–54 to make such formulations as *'the state it has won is dependent on imperialism and is a satellite state'*, *'in the new state, therefore the national bourgeoisie shares power with imperialism, with the latter still dominant indirectly'*, *'the Mountabatten award does not really signify a retreat of imperialism, but its cunning counter-offensive'*, etc., in the Political *Thesis* of the Second Congress. Again, even in the 1951 Party Programme, which attempted to correct the sectarian mistakes of the Second Congress Thesis, formulations such as *'the key part of our independence is still left in the hands of British* imperialism', *'the government is subservient to British imperialists'*, and *'the government of India essentially carries out the foreign policy of British imperialism'*, etc., were made in plenty.

The running thread and the theme of all these formulations was, mainly, to lay on thick the idea that Indian independence was 'formal' and thus to reject the new status of India as of either 'political independence' or 'national independence'.

Another serious mistake behind this view also lies in the over-simplified notion that there cannot be any political independence as long as economic dependence remains, and hence it cannot but be formal independence. Such a view emanates from the mistaken idea that what counts is only the economic factor, almost to the exclusion of the political factor – a sort of economic determinism – which itself is wrong. And even while stressing the economic factor, these comrades take a one-sided view seeing only the extent and operation of foreign capital in the country almost totally discounting Indian capital including big capital, and the opportunities it has of utilizing the political independence that has been won, the state power in its hands, to strengthen its bargaining position vis-à-vis foreign capital. The left-sectarian mistake arises from ignoring the interaction between the economic and political factors and a one-sided view of the role of foreign capital alone in the economy shutting one's eyes to the existence of Indian capital, its conflicts and contradictions with foreign capital in the very orbit of collaboration with it.

What has life proved and our own experience demonstrated? Several developments in the life of our country, subsequent to these generalisations of ours in our resolutions and documents, come up against such a left-sectarian understanding.

The speedy recognition of People's China, the signing of the Tibet agreement with People's China and the joint declaration of Panch Sheel, the development of friendly and closer relations with the Soviet Union and China, the role played at the Bandung conference, the increased stress on world peace against the imperialist war menace, the participation in the Korean armistice and the 1954 Geneva agreement, the readiness to go in for Soviet assistance for industry and trade, the embarking on ambitious industrial planning, etc., by the Indian government could not be explained in terms of 'formal independence', 'satellite state', 'puppet government' and the like. Events proved that imperialism was not that powerful to be able to reduce our national independence to formal independence, and the new Indian state and government could assert in certain measure, its political independence – thanks to the new world correlation of forces that came into existence following the second world war.

In India, however distorted and however restricted, parliamentary democracy based on adult franchise still exists, showing that the Indian ruling classes have still a social base. This is not possible for any puppet state or government whose ruling classes cannot have such a social base in the country, are so totally isolated from the entire people that they can continue their existence only with the help of imperialist bayonets.

Our Party, drawing on its own experience and learning from its earlier sectarian mistakes, discarded the concept of 'formal independence', and incorporated its correct understanding in the new Party Programme. The opening chapter itself begins with the caption, 'India attains national independence' and concludes its analysis thus: 'As a result, the country was partitioned into India and Pakistan, and political power was transferred to the leaders of the Congress party on August 15, 1947. Thus ended the political rule of the British in India and a state headed by the Indian big bourgeoisie was established. With this the first stage of the Indian revolution, the stage of general national united front, chiefly directed against foreign imperialist rule came to an end.'

'The British imperialists hoped that, despite the transfer of power, they would be able, by their entrenched positions, in our economy, to make our independence *formal*. But the course of historical development since then has been, disappointing to the imperialists and their hopes were belied.' (*Party Programme* Paras 3 and 4)

Thus the Party Programme decisively rejected the pet theme of 'formal independence' with which we played for a time in our Party to the detriment of our working out a correct strategy and tactical line. One does not know why these comrades once again toy with the slogan of 'formal independence'.

It is amazing that they do not bother to explain the grounds on which they come to this conclusion and demand revision of the Programme on this score. They simply cite certain facts of economic collaboration with foreign capital, the resulting dependence from such collaboration, and go to deduce from it their thesis of 'surrender to imperialism' and 'independence getting formal'.

The Party Programme takes due note of the role of foreign capital in our national economy and points out as to how 'the rapid growth of U.S. investments in certain key sectors brings to the forefront the growing danger of American penetration into our economy and consequently political life' and how despite the assistance got from socialist countries and 'despite the fact that Indian capital has grown in volume, the most glaring fact of our economic life today is that the country's economy as a whole is in many respects precariously dependent on western assistance particularly U.S. assistance.' (*Party Programme*, Paras 24, 25 and 26)

And yet the Programme did not draw the conclusion of 'formal independence', and a 'puppet state'.

To judge whether the independence of a country is formal or otherwise a number of economic, political, national, and international factors have to be taken into account: the simple fact that several countries and states today are economically dependent upon one imperialism or the other, and that their bourgeois governments are collaborating with foreign capital in some measure or other does in no way signify that they have become 'formally independent' and 'satellite states'. To say so is, to put it mildly, over-simplification par excellence.

IS THE INDIAN BIG BOURGEOISIE COMPRADOR?

On this issue there never was a controversy inside the Communist movement in India, as everybody accepted the analysis made by the Sixth Congress of the C.I. on this question. It was only raised by the Chinese Communist Party, for the first time, in 1960, in its articles 'On Nehru's Philosophy' and 'Once More on Nehru's Philosophy'. The attention of the Drafting Committee and other leading comrades was drawn to these new Chinese references. After careful consideration it was rejected as incorrect. None in our Party, either at the stage of the pre-Congress discussions or during the Seventh Congress discussions raised any objection on this issue, even though many had read the Chinese documents. Neither at the Congress nor during the last forty months since the Party Congress has any leading comrade or any party unit raised any controversy over this question, except, in the recent months, by the extremist leaders of the Naxalbari platform, vigorously backed by the Chinese radio and press. Our critics unfortunately uphold this position and maintain that the Chinese criticism of our Party is essentially correct. Hence a thorough discussion of the subject is required so as to leave no scope for confusion on this score.

The first thing that we should be clear about is what exactly is meant by the term comprador bourgeoisie, before we proceed to discuss whether the Indian big bourgeoisie is in the main of a comprador character or not.

The Thesis of the Sixth Congress of the C.I. describes the comprador bourgeoisie as 'native merchants, engaged in trade with imperialist centres, whose interests are in continuation of imperialist exploitation. They act as agents for exploiting the masses in the colonial countries.' Also, 'a definite comprador position, a position of intermediary trader, sub-exploiter or overseer over the enslaved population.'

The same Thesis states: 'The national bourgeoisie in these colonial countries does not adopt a uniform attitude in relation to imperialism. A part of this bourgeoisie, more especially the trading bourgeoisie, directly serves the interests of imperialist capital (the so-called comprador bourgeoisie). In general, it more or less consistently defends the anti-national imperialist point of view directed against the whole nationalist movement, in common with the feudal allies of imperialism and the more highly paid native officials'.

Further, 'The remaining portions of the native bourgeoisie, especially the portion reflecting the interests of native industry, support the national movement and represent a special vacillating, compromising tendency which may be designated as national reformism (or, in the terminology of the Thesis of the Second Congress of the Communist International, a 'bourgeois-democratic' tendency)'.

Dealing with the specific character of the bourgeoisie in China and India among other colonial and semi-colonial countries, the Thesis proceeds: 'This intermediate position of the national bourgeoisie between the revolutionary and imperialist camps is no longer to be observed, it is true, in China after 1925; there the greater part of the national bourgeoisie from the beginning, owing to the special situation, took the leadership in the national emancipatory war; later on it passed over finally into the camp of counterrevolution. In India and Egypt, we still observe, for the time being, the typical bourgeois-nationalist movement – an opportunist movement, subject to great vacillations, balancing between imperialism and revolution'.

How do earlier Chinese communist writings define the comprador bourgeoisie?

'A comprador in the original sense of the word, was the Chinese manager or senior office employee in a foreign commercial establishment. The comprador served foreign economic interests and had close connections with imperialism and foreign capital'. (Mao Tse-tung, *Selected Works*, Peking Edition, Vol. I, p. 19)

'In economically backward and semi-colonial China the landlord class and the comprador class are wholly appendages of the imperialist bourgeoisie depending upon imperialism for their survival and growth. These classes represent the most backward and most reactionary relations of production in China and hinder the development of her productive forces. Their existence is utterly incompatible with the aims of the Chinese revolution. The big landlords and big comprador classes in particular always side with imperialism and constitute an extreme counter-revolutionary group'. (*Ibid*, p. 14)

'The Chinese big bourgeoisie, which is comprador in character, is a class which directly serves imperialism and is fostered by it. Hence the comprador Chinese big bourgeoisie has always been the target of revolution'. (Mao Tse-tung, *Selected Works*, Vol. II, p. 289)

How did the Chinese Communist Party distinguish between sections of the bourgeois class of China? It defined the bourgeoisie in two categories according to their role in social production and their economic and political status, one as the comprador big bourgeoisie and the other as the national bourgeoisie which in the main is the middle bourgeoisie.

'There is a distinction between the comprador big bourgeoisie and national bourgeoisie.

'The comprador big bourgeoisie is a class which directly serves the capitalists of the imperialist countries and is nurtured by them . . . . Therefore it is a target of the Chinese revolution and never in the history of the revolution has it been a motive force . . . .

'The national bourgeoisie in China, which is mainly the middle bourgeoisie has never really held political power but has been restricted by the reactionary policies of the big landlord class and big bourgeoisie which are in power, although it followed them in opposing the revolution in the period from 1927 to 1931', etc. (Mao Tse-tung, *Selected Works*, Vol. II, pp. 320–21).

We have quoted these passages at length in order to leave no room for any confusion, as to what the exact position of the C.I. and the Chinese Communist Party was regarding the definition of comprador bourgeoisie and its attitude to imperialism and the national liberation movement.

What emerges from all this is that the comprador and non-comprador sections of the bourgeoisie have their own distinct characteristics and it will be a grievous error to mix them up.

The comprador bourgeoisie in a colonial, dependent or backward country is a servitor of foreign imperialism concerned mainly with trade operations connected with the export of indigenous raw materials and the import of manufactured goods from imperialist countries as well as credit and moneylending dealings. They do not represent native capitalist production, in fact stand in its way. It is through these representatives of primitive forms of capital that imperialism carries on the trade and moneylending and banking exploitation of the enslaved peoples of the colonies.

In contrast, the non-comprador bourgeoisie has capitalist

production as the base of its existence and is the spokesman for the development of indigenous capitalist production. It is active in the spheres of industrial production, of trade and of banking, lives by appropriating surplus value from the exploitation of wage-labour. As such, it is only natural that the capitalist ambitions of the non-comprador bourgeoisie come into conflict with imperialism though it is tied by innumerable strings to the foreign monopolists.

The comprador bourgeoisie is always in the camp of imperialism and has no contradiction with the imperialism it serves, while the non-comprador section has its conflicts and contradictions with imperialism, though even this section of the bourgeoisie always seeks to solve these contradictions through compromise. All this should be crystal clear to any Marxist-Leninist.

With this understanding let us examine concretely how things stand with the Indian bourgeois class, how the C.I. analysed it, how our Party has based itself on the C.I. analysis and how our Party Programme takes its stand on the issue.

First of all, the C.I. held the opinion that India was the most capitalistically developed among all the colonial and semi-colonial countries in the period under examination, i.e., the 1920–30's. This point was emphasised again and again by several C.I. documents, Stalin and other communist writers of that period.

Secondly, the Indian big bourgeoisie was divided by the C.I. into two main categories, one comprador and the other industrial, and while the former was always supporting the imperialists and feudal reaction, the latter was reflecting the interests of native industry and supporting the national movement, and representing national reformism. The leadership of the Indian National Congress was always representing in the main the industrial bourgeoisie of India and was in their service.

Thirdly, this industrial big bourgeoisie of India which got additionally strengthened during the years of the second world war and after, and which was represented by the Congress, came into the leadership of the new state and government following the transfer of power in August 1947. Fourthly, the big comprador section in India, which at one stage was acting as the ally of foreign imperialism and native landlordism against the national movement, is today neither in the same condition nor in a position to play the same role. Several of them, during the last 30 years, have set up certain industries and grown into, mainly, the industrial category. Today the great bulk of the big bourgeoisie represents, in the main, the industrial big bourgeoisie. Foreign imperialists, today, do not depend on their alliance with the comprador class for the perpetuation of their positions in India, as in the past, but, mainly, depend upon the big industrial bourgeoisie, which is in the leadership of the state power, for the protection of their interests, though economic collaboration with foreign capital is not, principally, collaboration in business and trade with the imperialists, as was the case with the big commercial and trading bourgeoisie which was mainly interested in sharing the commission on imports and exports along with the imperialists. The industrial collaboration between the bourgeoisie of India and foreign capitalists should not be equated with comprador collaboration with the foreign imperialists. To do so would be grievously wrong since the roles of these two respective sections of the big bourgeoisie in the social production relations fundamentally differ and their respective stakes in the country's industrial production, too, fundamentally vary. The comprador class, as a parasitic class, has no conflict and contradiction with the imperialists, only complete and total subservience to and abject dependence on foreign capitalists. Whereas the industrial big bourgeois class, despite its capitalist path of industrialisation, has also some conflicts and contradictions with the foreign imperialists, which, of course, it seeks to resolve by using its newly acquired state power. This is pointed out in the Programme thus: 'it seeks to utilise its hold over the state and the new opportunities to strengthen its position by attacking the people on the one hand and, on the other, to resolve the conflicts and contradictions with imperialism and feudalism by pressure, bargain and compromise'. (*Party Programme*, Para 15)

This is not just one casual mention made in our Party Programme, there are others. To quote a few:

> 1. 'Our country, even while it was under the colonial rule of the British, was one of the capitalistically developed colonies and semi-colonies. The big bourgeoisie which headed the national liberation movement and the new independent state after 1947 has been continuously in state power for nearly two decades and has been utilising that state power to immensely strengthen its

class position at the expense of the mass of people on the one hand and compromising and bargaining with imperialism and big landlordism on the other'. (Para 85)

2. 'The working class and the Communist Party does take cognisance of the contradictions and conflicts that do exist between the Indian bourgeoisie, including the big bourgeoisie, and foreign imperialists. They express themselves on the issues of war and peace, on the economic and, political relations with socialist countries, on the terms of aid from foreign monopolists, on the question of finding adequate markets for our exports, and on the question of foreign policy and defence of our national independence. In the background of the daily intensifying general crisis of world capitalism, the different contradictions obtaining in the national and international spheres are bound to get intensified. The Communist Party, while carefully studying this phenomenon, shall strive to utilise every such difference, fissure, conflict and contradiction with the foreign imperialists to isolate the imperialists and strengthen the people's struggle for democratic advance. Entertaining no illusion of any strategic unity or united front with the ruling Congress party, the working class will not hesitate to lend its unstinted support to the government on all issues of world peace and anti-colonialism which are in the genuine interests of the nation, on all economic and political issues of conflict with imperialism, and on all issues which involve questions of strengthening our sovereignty and independent foreign policy'. (Para 108)

3. 'The Indian bourgeoisie as a class, coming as it is from an underdeveloped and newly liberated country as ours, has its conflicts and contradictions with imperialism and also with the feudal and the semi-feudal agrarian order. But the bigger and monopoly section, after attainment of independence, seeks to utilise its hold over the state power to resolve these conflicts and contradictions by compromise, pressure and bargain'. (Para 105)

Then, is it not amazing that in the face of this clear and unambiguous position taken in the Party Programme about the class character and nature of the Indian big bourgeoisie, some comrades frontally challenge its entire basis and argue that the Chinese criticism on this score is essentially correct, that the Indian big bourgeoisie is comprador and its comprador character is growing?

Here again, it is regrettable that they neither care to define what the comprador class is, nor bother to analyse the Indian big bourgeoisie and prove its comprador character. They do not even pause for a while before attacking the programmatic foundations to look back on the entire history of our Party on this issue and the analysis of the C.I. on the same.

How do they wish to substantiate their contention?

1. 'Majority of our industries, both in the public and private sectors, especially the industries of the collaborating big business, are *completely foreign orientated*'.

What this 'majority' is and what 'completely foreign orientated' is, we have yet to hear from the authors! But if one were to talk on the basis of facts, such statements are to be characterised as grossly subjective and exaggerated.

2. 'Of late, establishment of joint industries where western capitalists have come to dominate'.

3. Because of the growing economic crisis and slump in the internal market 'Indian big business is forced to try for external market in collaboration with foreign imperialists'.

'Because of the above reasons, the collaborating big business, is acquiring a marked comprador nature,' etc.

The first two reasons advanced above in support of their case are the economic and industrial collaboration of Indian big business with foreign capital. On this aspect our Party Programme and several other resolutions speak more eloquently and with far greater and concrete facts and figures. May we know from these comrades how, from this economic and industrial collaboration, the comprador character can be straightaway deduced? If economic and political terminology we use has any meaning, is it not clumsily confusing the concepts of industrial and comprador sections? Why resort to this method and derail the discussions into absolutely wrong channels?

Then, as to the third reason adduced, it goes diametrically against their thesis, as it is a case of the industrial bourgeoisie seeking collaboration with the imperialists for selling their industrial produce. How does it prove the comprador character and negate their industrial nature? We are compelled to conclude that the critics again are badly confused in understanding the clear meaning of the term 'collaborationist bourgeoisie' and 'comprador bourgeoisie'.

If the argument they advocate, 'Indian big business is forced to try for external market in collaboration with foreign imperialists', is to be taken seriously, then the question stands on a totally different footing, viz., the big bourgeoisie producing goods in the country and trying to market those goods in world markets with imperialist help. Then it is a clear case of a producing industrial bourgeoisie trying to sell their goods and earn profits, but cannot be a comprador or trading bourgeoisie who, in the main, act as salesmen and commission agents of the imperialists, to push the sale of their goods in the colonial market. One is at a loss to understand the logic behind the argument!

What is the actual reality? The interests of all the industrial bourgeoisie of newly liberated and underdeveloped countries, irrespective of their degree of economic dependence and economic collaboration with foreign capital, demand protective tariffs and import restrictions in their countries, against the dumping of goods by foreign capitalists. This element is an element of conflict with the imperialists, notwithstanding economic collaboration. Similarly, the imperialists close their markets for the manufactured goods of the underdeveloped countries, if any, and force them to undersell their raw-produce utilising their stronger position and monopoly. This again is an element of conflict and contradiction between the bourgeoisie of backward states and the imperialists. In fact, what stands out glaringly from the discussions, in the recent meetings of UNCTAD and the oft-repeated outcries about 'have-nations' squeezing out the 'have-not nations', is the above pointed conflicts and contradictions. It is really astounding that our critics not only miss this aspect clean and exclusively highlight the collaboration aspect in this regard, but go further and deduce from it the absurd conclusion, that it is the comprador character of Indian big business that is behind all this!

These comrades do not seem to be interested in arguing their case cogently on the basis of concrete facts and realities. What they are resorting to is different. They are trying, by hook or by crook, to justify their thesis that the Indian Government is a puppet of the USA, that

Indian independence is formal and bogus and what we have in India today is a neo-colonial state, not a bourgeois-landlord state led by the big bourgeoisie which is collaborating with foreign capital and allying with landlordism to pursue its capitalist path. As a short-cut to prove their thesis, they invent a comprador character in the Indian big bourgeoisie, consider it as the predominant element, and on that basis weave out the thesis that since Indian big business is a parasitic, trading and commercial class, totally dependent upon imperialists for its existence and growth, they are lackeys of U.S. imperialism, and the state they are in power of is a neo-colonial state with a puppet government, etc.

Comrades who simply cite the Chinese analogy to prove their contention of the comprador character of the Indian big bourgeoisie, do not think it necessary to go into the concrete facts of capitalist development in present-day India when compared with pre-revolutionary China. Nor do they analyse the historical and political reasons as to why this difference in the development of capitalism and modern industry between India and pre-revolutionary China did come about. They go by only drawing parallels and analogies.

Comrade Mao, describing the Chinese capitalist development and the growth of the modern working class, in the year 1926, states thus: 'The modern industrial proletariat numbers about two million. It is not large because China is economically backward. These two million industrial workers are mainly employed in five industries – railways, mining, maritime and transport, textiles and ship building – *and a great number are enslaved in enterprises owned by foreign capitalists*'. (*Selected Works*, Vol. I, p. 8 – Emphasis ours)

Again touching on the same topic in the year 1935, Mao observes: 'Among the Chinese proletariat, the modern industrial workers number from 2,500,000 to 3,000,000, the workers in small-scale industry and in handicraft and the shop assistants in the cities total about 12,000,000, and in addition there are great numbers of rural proletarians (the farm labourers) and other propertyless people in the cities and the countryside'. (*Selected Works*, Vol. II, p. 324).

All this brings out, first, that the five industries mentioned above were the main industries in China, and the total employment did not exceed two to three million workers. Secondly, most of those industries were owned by foreign capitalists.

How do things stand with India?

As far as India is concerned, it was estimated that, as early as 1905, a daily average of 196,369 persons were employed in cotton textile mills and 133,162 in jute mills. The total factory labour in India stood around two million by 1905. As many as 1494 joint stock companies were registered in India by the year 1905, with a paid-up capital of Rs. 48 crores.

R. Palme Dutt, in his *India Today*, concludes from the Industrial Census and Census of India statistics that 'In the narrower sense of the industrial proletariat in modern or other than petty industry, the Industrial Census of 1921 reached a total of 2.6 million employed in establishments employing ten or more workers. There has been no later Industrial Census; but the estimate of the 1931 Census, given above, would place the total at about $3^1/_2$ millions . . . .

These $3^1/_2$ million represent the kernel of the industrial proletariat in modern large-scale industry in India today. Excluded from the total are all the workers in petty industry (establishments under ten workers), as well as in larger enterprises without power-driven machinery (e.g., cigarette making, with, in some cases, over fifty workers). From the standpoint of the potential strength of the organised labour movement, we should add the over one million workers employed on the plantations, who are employed in fully large-scale enterprise under the most scientific slave-driving conditions . . . . and a proportion of the workers in petty industry and the larger unregulated enterprises. The immediate effective organisable strength of the Indian working class should therefore certainly represent over five million workers'.

As for the total strength of the Indian working class, 'persons employed in plantations, mines, industry and transport', Dutt quotes the 1931 Census Report as recording that this strength 'in 1921 was 24,239,555, of whom only 2,685,909 were employed in organised establishments employing ten or more employees' and 'total figure under the same heads in 1931 amounts to 26,187,689'.

More than three decades have passed since then, during which there was the second world war with the consequent new opportunities for industrial development in India and the twenty years of post-independence development, both deserving special mention. Powerful industrial houses and monopolists have grown controlling the major part of industry and banking. Today Indian capital in industry has increased by sixty times compared to the year 1905 and stands around Rs. 3,000 crores.

All this does not concern our comrades. They insist and maintain that the conditions in pre-revolutionary China and present-day India are more or less the same.

That all the colonies and dependent countries did not belong to the same category was clear to the Communist International in the early twenties itself. Stalin, in his speech delivered at a meeting of the students of the University of the Peoples of the East on May 18, 1925, said, 'Thirdly, in certain of these countries, India, for instance, capitalism is growing very rapidly and is engendering and causing to crystallise a more or less numerous class of native proletarians'. Further, he says, 'In earlier days the colonial East was pictured as something single and homogeneous. This picture no longer corresponds to the truth. We have now at least three categories of colonies and dependent countries. Firstly, there are countries like Morocco, which have no proletariat or almost no proletariat, and which industrially are completely undeveloped. Secondly, there are countries like China and Egypt, which are industrially little developed and which have a comparatively small proletariat. Thirdly, there are countries like India, which are capitalistically more or less developed, and which possess a more or less numerous national proletariat'. To emphasise the point again, Stalin stresses, 'Clearly, it is quite impossible to put all these countries in the same category'.

With all this it should be quite clear that our comrades are not interested in making any concrete analysis but are interested only in fitting facts into their preconceived conclusions.

Is it not utter blindness to ignore all this and draw mechanical analogies with pre-revolutionary China, and try to prove that the Indian big bourgeoisie, in the main, is comprador and not industrial?

It is one thing to point out how this industrial development is insignificant compared to the needs, times and possibilities. Similarly it is also correct to sharply point out how this industrial development through dependence and collaboration with foreign capital can never achieve the industrial revolution, that, on the other hand, it endangers national independence. This exactly is what we have done in our Programme, showing, how a People's Democratic revolution alone is the way out to overcome these maladies. But invention of facts like 'comprador class' in the leadership of state and government in the present-day India to suit one's subjective thesis of a 'puppet regime' is fantastic in the extreme.

Before concluding this topic of controversy regarding the alleged comprador character of the Indian big bourgeoisie we would like to draw the attention of party members to certain other statements made by our critics.

They state that, 'after 1958–59, the economic dependence of our country under the present government is growing apace'. Does it imply that prior to 1958–59, our country was economically more independent? Or do they mean to suggest that the needs of the Indian bourgeoisie for seeking greater economic aid and collaboration with foreign capital, in pursuit of their capitalist path, have further increased, and consequently internal and external policies are being adjusted to these needs? One cannot clearly understand the argument. At any rate we are unable to appreciate this logic, because even granting that the dependence is growing apace, as fast as they conceive, how does it prove the growing comprador character of the monopolists? We know from history, of sections of comprador bourgeoisie, smaller or bigger in number depending upon several factors, evolving into the industrial category. This is what took place in India, and probably with the other big bourgeoisie of some colonial and semi-colonial countries. But we are yet to know of the reverse course of an industrial big bourgeoisie of a backward and underdeveloped state evolving into a comprador category. These comrades clearly suggest this reverse process, and argue that Indian 'big business is acquiring a marked comprador nature' since 1958–59, and that the Central Committee is guilty of failing to 'see this growing comprador nature of big business'.

It follows from all their arguments that they treat the terms 'comprador', 'collaboration', 'dependence' as one and the same thing. If such is the case, a free and fair discussion on the topic becomes impossible and clarity on the issues unattainable.

NEO-COLONIAL STATE AND PUPPET GOVERNMENT

The political platform of Naxalbari, set up by the extremist rebels, which is getting massive support from the Peking radio and Chinese press, has been vigorously putting across this concept of 'neo-colonial state' and 'puppet government' to oppose our Party Programme and political line. It is true that these comrades nowhere formulate it so clearly and categorically. But all the arguments like 'formal independence', 'comprador class in power', etc., are being forcefully advanced, as examined and pointed out above. On top of it, they assert that the Chinese radio and press criticism of our Party is 'essentially correct on all these points'. What this characterisation of 'neo-colonial state', etc., boils down to, needs closer analysis and examination.

It is an admitted fact that our Party Programme has sharply pointed out that the massive economic collaboration with foreign capital would endanger our political independence. Again, in *New Situation and Party's Tasks*, after exposing the government's anti-people policies, it is stated that, 'unless these policies of the Congress government are totally defeated, the country is in for neo-colonialist domination by the USA' (p. 22).

To expose the menacing consequences of economic collaboration with foreign capital, especially with that of the USA, and rouse class and mass opinion against the impending danger of neo-colonialist domination is very necessary, and what our Party is doing is exactly that. But it is one thing to point out the danger and quite another thing to state that neo-colonial conquest of our country by the U.S. is already an accomplished fact.

To prove the thesis of a 'neo-colonial state and puppet government', certain facts of economic collaboration and dependence for aid on the U.S. imperialists by the Indian government and instances of consequent tuning of the foreign policy emasculating the declared aims of non-alignment are cited. If economic collaboration and the pursuit of a policy that abets the U.S. imperialists in one measure or other is the sole criterion to decide that a particular state and government is 'neo-colonial and puppet', then we slip into a totally erroneous conclusion that most of the capitalist states and governments in the world are neo-colonial states, with stooge governments under U.S. imperialism, because these two factors are present, in one degree or other, in most of those states and governments. There are different degrees of economic collaboration and dependence, different degrees of acquiescing in or abetting or actively supporting the aggressive policies of the U.S., as also different degrees of opposition to the U.S. by these states. Without going into a concrete study of all the relevant factors, it is dangerous to take a brush and tar them all as 'neo-colonial states'. The case of France from advanced capitalist states, and of Pakistan from the newly liberated countries which were once rightly considered as appendages of the U.S. and members of the NATO and SEATO aggressive war-blocs – which they, of course, formally continue to be even now – clearly refute such a theory of a neo-colonial state, merely on the basis of economic dependence and collaboration.

Neo-colonialism is an art long practised by the U.S. imperialists, mainly in Latin American countries and states. They are states where not only economic collaboration with and economic dependence on the U.S. monopolists are present, but all the main arteries of economic life are either owned, controlled or directed by the U.S., the major part of the industries are run for the U.S., the bourgeois-democratic rights and liberties are annulled, and rule by military juntas is established, which rule is again wholly dependent on the direct military support of the USA. The big bourgeois leaders of these states have sold themselves, heart and soul, to U.S. imperialists by accepting some crumbs from the U.S. monopolists, have become junior partners, and can remain in power only by the consent of the U.S. magnates. The bloc vote that the U.S. mobilises in the present UNO is from these satellites.

Can anybody seriously suggest that these very same conditions exist in present-day India though we fundamentally oppose the present bourgeois-landlord state and government of India? The country's economic and political conditions, the respective hold and control of the country's economic life by the local big bourgeoisie and foreign capitalists, and several other factors in our country basically differ from those of the neo-colonial states in Latin America. To refuse to take into account concrete facts and look only for easy analogies can never be the attitude of a serious Marxist-Leninist.

It is perfectly true that the U.S. imperialists are making hectic attempts to create a neo-colonial world empire on the ruins of the old colonialism in the post-second world war period. But it is neither easy for them to succeed in this, nor is the present-day world so pliable as to allow such an easy victory. Such attempts in South Korea, South Vietnam, Philippines, etc., have resulted in directly manning these states with massive occupation forces with all the consequent results, i.e., instead of neo-colonialism, the most aggressive colonialism that tops the old colonialism has come to prevail. The neo-colonial experiment has not succeeded with Pakistan. In the face of many such realities, we are at a loss to understand, as to why certain comrades jump to the sweeping conclusion that the U.S. has already succeeded in its job of reducing India to the status of its neo-colony, and that the Indian big bourgeoisie has become so isolated and frightened by class revolution as to accept abject surrender to the U.S. Such a view, in one sense, discounts the popular forces in the country as also the new correlation of world forces favourable to the people. Such a view so exaggerates the growth and sharpening of the contradiction between the people and the government as to take it to the point of an imminent threat of class revolution, it so exaggerates the depth and maturity of the contradiction between U.S. imperialism and our country as to make it the principal contradiction in our national scene. Such a view totally discounts the operation of inner-imperialist contradictions and the contradiction between the socialist camp and imperialist camp and their operation in India, the single biggest backward and under-developed country in the world. All this results in rejecting the characterisation of the stage and strategy given in our Party Programme. To define the present Indian state as a neo-colonial state of the U.S. will have no meaning whatsoever, if its social implications for the revolutionary movement are not drawn.

CONTRADICTIONS IN OUR SOCIETY

In the situation obtaining in our country at the present stage what are the main contradictions? The contradiction between feudal landlordism and the mass of peasantry, the contradiction between imperialism and the nation and the contradiction between the working class and the bourgeoisie – these are the three basic contradictions present in the process.

What is the principal contradiction out of these three?

The Programme maintains that the contradiction between big landlordism and the mass of the peasantry is the principal contradiction, which in political terms expresses itself as the contradiction between the present bourgeois-landlord state and government and the vast bulk of the people. This is the position after the attainment of political independence.

What was the principal contradiction in the previous period when British occupation and rule existed?

The Programme maintains that the contradiction between British imperialism and the nation was the principal one.

Do our critics agree with this or not?

They do not directly answer it, but by devious arguments they reject it. The thesis that ours is a neo-colonial state under U.S. imperialism with a stooge government headed by a comprador class obviously means that the U.S. imperialists are the real and actual rulers, that the Indian state is a state run by them through their Indian lackeys, that the present neo-colonial rule by U.S. is a substitute to the old colonial rule by the British, and that in substance nothing has changed except changing of hands from the British to the U.S.

Does all this signify something in terms of contradictions? It cannot but do so, and that is, the contradiction between the U.S. and its Indian lackeys on the one hand, and the entire nation on the other, is so accentuated as to assume the principal role among the contradictions in the process.

What follows necessarily from such an assessment? First, the stage of the revolution, instead of being democratic or agrarian as the Programme lays down, becomes the stage of a general national united front, directing its edge mainly against foreign imperialism, the U.S. Secondly, as a consequence, not only the class strategy and tactics but also the agrarian programme will have to undergo a change.

But the advocates of the theory of a 'neo-colonial state' dare not openly say it. They only shout about the total surrender and subservience to U.S. domination but refuse to concretise it in terms of contradictions and the change in their position to create a new situation that is radically different from the one where national independence exists.

A Marxist-Leninist method of serious study, investigation, analysis and assessment is different from what these comrades adopt.

Do our left critics, who maintain that the Indian big bourgeoisie is a comprador class enlighten us as to whether this *entire* stratum in India is exclusively dependent upon and in the service of U.S. imperialism, and if so, since when?

Do they agree that inter-imperialist contradictions, particularly, between the U.S. and Britain, not only exist and operate on the Indian soil, but also get accentuated? If so, has it any impact on the situation in our country, especially when the U.S., according to them, has succeeded in reducing India to the status of its neo-colony?

Do they agree with the Chinese Communist Party's statement that, 'these *massive U.S. imperialist inroads* represent an important step taken by the U.S. reactionaries in their *neo-colonialist plans* for India; they are an important development in the present overt and covert struggle among the imperialist countries to seize markets and spheres of influence and redivide the world. This U.S. action is bound to hasten a new awakening of the Indian people, and at the same time to *intensify the contradiction between British and U.S. imperialism in India*'. (*More on Differences with Togliatti.*)

The above statement speaks of '*massive U.S. inroads*' and '*neo-colonial plans for India*' by the U.S., and does not talk of India being already reduced to a 'neo-colonial state'. This was made in the year 1963. Can our left critics substantiate with facts that this process has been completed, unhindered, during the last four years?

The mere hurling of a phrase like 'neo-colonial state' does not lead us anywhere until its political bearing on our revolutionary struggle is seen and worked out. Comrade Mao did not satisfy himself with such sweeping characterisations, but described, in detail, the Chinese society during the period when the Japanese attack was on, as 'colonial, semi-colonial and *semi feudal society*', and on this basis worked out the strategy and tactics of the Chinese revolution.

The advocates of the 'neo-colonial state' thesis with a gusto argue that because of the growing crisis of the Indian economy and the ruling Congress party, and because of the growing world capitalist crisis and U.S. crisis, 'U.S. pressures are acting as real causes for the growing surrender of the Indian government to U.S. imperialism'.

Thus, only two factors are operating, according to them. The growing U.S. crisis and its pressure on the Indian government and the growing crisis and increasing surrender to U.S.! No contradictions exist between the U.S. and Indian big bourgeoisie, nor has the crisis any bearing on these contradictions; no inter-imperialist contradictions operate on the Indian scene; nor is it possible for the Indian bourgeoisie to try any measure to utilise them in their favour; no contradiction exists between the socialist and imperialist camps nor is its utilisation by the bourgeoisie, in some measure or other, possible. Only one process is in operation, viz., the march of the U.S. neo-colonial colossus and its comprador lackeys of the Indian government! Is it, then, any wonder that they arrive at their erroneous conclusions?

When the Central Committee says that the Indian big bourgeoisie will also try to utilise the different world contradictions in its favour, that it seeks to utilise Soviet aid to buttress its positions, and the growing crisis will also intensify the contradictions between the imperialists and the Indian bourgeoisie, these comrades dismiss it as totally wrong, asserting that they 'completely disagree with such an evaluation' since, according to them, 'this is a very superficial view of things'. Whose is the 'superficial' analysis and assessment – that of the Central Committee or that of these comrades? It is not difficult to judge.

As far as the Central Committee is concerned, it is intent on learning from the past mistakes of our Party. It is relevant to mention here how Comrade Mao exhorts the Communists to make serious investigations and study and emphasises the need for concrete analysis of concrete conditions. 'Lenin meant just this when he said that the most essential thing in Marxism, the living soul of Marxism, is the concrete analysis of concrete conditions. Our dogmatists have violated Lenin's teachings; they never use their brains to analyse anything concretely,' etc. 'Our dogmatists are lazy-bones. They refuse to undertake any painstaking study of concrete things, they regard general truths as emerging out of the void, they turn them into purely abstract unfathomable formulas, and thereby completely deny and reverse the normal sequence by which man comes to know truth'. (*On Contradictions*)

If our Central Committee is condemned for honestly attempting to apply these correct Marxist postulates to our situation, we do plead guilty to such a crime.

Before proceeding to examine the nature and contents of the attacks on the Party's line on the current situation, we wish to draw the attention of our Party comrades to certain facts regarding the background on which the *New Situation and Party's Tasks* is based.

This resolution of the Central Committee, in April 1967, is nothing but a consistent application and continuation of the political line decided at the Seventh Congress. The only attempt, made in it, is to reassess the post-general-election situation in the country and declare the tasks of our Party in accordance with the political line laid down at the Party Congress. The slogan of breaking the monopoly rule of the Congress, the slogan of non-Congress democratic alternative governments in the states, the slogan of forging united fronts with the democratic parties including the Right Communist Party, the nature and character of centre-state relations, etc., were raised and discussed in several Party documents. The Political Resolution and Resolution on the Kerala Mid-Term Elections of the Party Congress, the resolutions on the Party's election tactics on the eve of the fourth general elections, the Election Manifesto and the like deal with these questions. But the critics bypass all this background of the *New Situation and Party's Tasks* and launch their surprise offensive on the political line. That, too, is being done several months after its adoption and implementation without raising any dissent or criticism all these months.

They oppose the C.C.'s assessment of the post-election situation; they reject the election tactics and united front tactics of the Party; they question and challenge the correctness of the slogan of alternative non-Congress, democratic governments and our participation in them; they repudiate the analysis of different contradictions – patent as well as latent in the Indian situation, as given in the resolution; they find fault with the analysis of centre-state conflicts, as made in the *New Situation and Party's Tasks*; and they consider the entire line as a line repudiating the revolutionary line of our Party and the adoption of reformism, revisionism and parliamentary cretinism. Thus their disagreement with and opposition to the *New Situation and Party's Tasks* is total and complete, as there is nothing common, according to them, between the line it expounds and the alternative line they advocate.

When such is the case, it would have been fair and proper of them to systematically take up the issues and expound their alternative views. The critics do not choose this method. They choose the method of sniping attacks on the Central Committee resolution. And they also resort to the method of quoting passages from the resolution out of context, of quoting mutilated sentences and clauses, and even omitting parts of the same clauses and sentences that do not suit their purpose. What prompts them to do so is not difficult to detect.

Let us reproduce here the main points of *New Situation and Party's Tasks* as summarised in the Central Committee's resolution on *Divergent Views between CPC and Our Party:*

'The economic crisis in the country is deepening and fast enveloping one sector after another of the nation's economy. Further, it has also extended to the political sphere and a political crisis has set in and is likely to mature with speed in the coming period, even though, at present, it is only in its initial stages . . .

'The bourgeois-landlord government, led by the big bourgeoisie, in its pursuit of the capitalist path of development, is depending and relying on foreign monopoly capital to come to its aid, and consequently, the threat to our national independence is growing. Unless the policies of compromise and collaboration pursued by the big bourgeois leadership of the state are resisted and decisively defeated in time, the danger of neo-colonialism stares us in the face.

'The crisis is causing growing mass discontent among the people, and mass protest actions, demonstrations, strikes and several, other forms of struggles are on the increase. It offers tremendous opportunities to the working class and its Communist Party to take big strides in building the class organisations of the people and in forging and consolidating the united front of different democratic classes to defeat the bourgeois-landlord government and its policies.

'The single biggest weakness in the whole situation is the deplorable state of the political level of the proletariat, its class consciousness, its organisation, and its unity with the other toiling masses, particularly the peasantry. Special note is taken of the fact how the Communist Party is very weak and even non-existent in the greater part of the country and how it is further menaced with the onslaught of revisionism organised in the shape of the Right Communist Party.

'The C.C. resolution warns the Party ranks against 'any attempt to over-rate or exaggerate the degree of its (crisis) depth and maturity', as 'it would lead us to grossly underestimate the immense reserves still at the disposal of the big bourgeois-landlord classes, the room to manoeuvre which they still possess, on the one hand, and to do everything in their power to disrupt and suppress the popular struggles on the other, to perpetuate their exploiting class rule'.

'Lastly, it emphasises the need for struggle to win over the masses to our Programme and political line, underlines the scope for the use of parliamentary and extra-parliamentary struggles in correct combination, analyses the character, scope and function of the non-Congress democratic state coalition governments in which our Party is functioning while sharply pointing out how they are to be treated 'as instruments of struggle in the hands of our people' and 'our participation in such governments as one specific form of struggle to win more and more people and more and more allies' for the People's Democratic Revolution, and urges on the Party to boldly lead the mass struggles'. (Pp. 12–14)

It is the duty of our critics to criticise or condemn these points and show the reasons why they do so. Instead, they resort to simply attacks on the basis of 'distorted quotes' from it on the one hand, and the citing of misleading quotations from Lenin in support of their contentions, on the other.

PARTY'S U.F. TACTICS AND THE CRITICS

These comrades denounce the tactics of our Party, and its participation in the Kerala and West Bengal state governments as, according to them, they are 'the so-called United front governments in partnership with known reactionary forces and revisionists', and 'of joining such governments in coalition with a definitely reactionary class character', etc. They denounce the tactics as 'Millerandism' and quote a long passage from Lenin in support of their contention; and they describe it as falling victims to parliamentary cretinism and cite again the authority of Lenin who is alleged to have described the bourgeois parliaments as nothing but talking shops, 'brothels', etc.

May we also know from them, granting that all these are 'definitely reactionary' parties, whether the formation of such fronts with them against the Congress party and government is forbidden by Marxism-Leninism of the new epoch? If so, can they enlighten us as to how the Chinese Communists could advocate a united front against Japanese imperialism with Chiang Kai-shek, the representative of the most reactionary comprador class in China? Or do they dispute the correctness of the Chinese statement in their well-known June 14th Letter that in the front against U.S. imperialism there will be not only workers, peasants, petty bourgeoisie and intellectuals 'but also patriotic national bourgeoisie and even certain kings, princes and aristocrats who are patriotic'? Does their patriotism and anti-U.S. stand wash off the reactionary class character of kings, princes, aristocrats and bourgeoisie?

Our Party has been consistently holding the opinion that the ruling Congress Party, which has been in possession of monopoly power over the bourgeois-landlord state in India, happens to be the principal political party of the most reactionary classes in India, and the major forces of these most reactionary classes and groups are rallied behind the Congress party. A struggle to isolate it and build a front or fronts in states against it with as many democratic parties and groups as possible, excluding the Swatantra, Jana Sangh and the like, is considered as a revolutionary task. Our yardstick is whether these tactics have been to the benefit of the proletariat or the bourgeoisie. If all this is dubbed as 'partnership with known reactionary forces' and denounced by our critics as opportunist tactics, it is they who find themselves in complete rupture with the party line and Marxist-Leninist tactics, but not the C.C. resolution, *New Situation and Party's Tasks.* Let them critically examine their stand, instead of slinging mud at the C.C. resolution and the Party's line on the current situation.

These comrades deliberately level a totally unfounded charge against the C.C. resolution, the charge that it is completely ignorant of the difference between state power and the non-Congress democratic governments in states like Kerala and West Bengal, and mount a big polemic against it. At the end of this 'profound' polemic they work themselves up and ask: 'Is it not against the teachings of Lenin who said that bourgeois parliaments are mere talking shops, are brothel houses where fraternity, equality and brotherhood are cheaply sold'?

Is this all that our comrades have learnt from Lenin, is this the Leninist teaching on the subject under discussion which they want to impart to the C.C.? Did not Lenin take up cudgels against the left-infantilism of those who were indulging in the frivolous talk of revolution and the demagogic denunciation of the utility of the bourgeois parliamentary forums? Better we remind our critics about this side of Lenin's teachings also. Otherwise, it would be gross distortion of Lenin to depict him as though he saw nothing more than 'mere talking shops and brothels' in bourgeois parliaments. The great Lenin also tells us that it is in the bourgeois 'parliament that the class relations between bourgeois parties and groups manifest themselves most frequently and reflect the relations between all the classes in the bourgeois society' and that 'Parliament is a scene of the class struggle'. Polemising against the left-infantile slogans of certain people who advocated boycott of parliament, on the ground that they are 'talking shops', Lenin tells them that different classes of people who are politically backward 'really think that their interests are represented in parliament' and 'this idea must be combated by work within parliament and by citing facts, so as to show the masses the truth'. He sums up, 'theory will have no effect on the backward masses; they need practical experience'.

Can our critics say that the advanced sections of the revolutionary classes, let alone the bulk of the still backward masses, in our country have come to such a stage as to understand the real class character of parliament? Or can they say that the revolutionary struggle has reached such a stage where basic issues are being decided in the open streets and in decisive class battles and the revolutionary representatives are betraying that struggle by participating in the parliamentary institutions, instead of participating in the street battles? If they say so they have to prove it by facts. If not, it would be tantamount to sheer phrase-mongering and nothing else.

The left critics in support of their case against the Party's tactics of united front's with other democratic parties in Kerala and West Bengal, refer to the following passage from Lenin's article on 'Marxism and Revisionism' written in the year 1908:

'The experience of alliances, agreements, and blocs with the social reform liberals in the west and liberal reformists (Cadets) in the Russian revolution, has convincingly shown that these agreements only blunt the consciousness of the masses, that they do not enhance but weaken the actual significance of their struggle by linking fights with elements who are least capable of fighting and most vacillating and treacherous. Millerandism in France – the biggest experiment in applying revisionist political tactics on a wide, really national scale   has provided a practical appraisal of revisionism that will never be forgotten by the proletariat all over the world.' (Lenin, *Against Revisionism*, p. 116)

We have pointed out just above how these comrades cite Lenin and his teachings on the attitude of the Marxists to bourgeois parliaments, and how it is totally distorted for their purpose.

Once again they are citing Lenin, and this time, too, with the same aim. We wish to draw their attention to another passage of Lenin in the same article which reads thus: 'And the 'revisionism from the left' which has begun to take shape in the Latin countries, such as 'revolutionary syndicalism' is also adapting itself to Marxism while 'amending' it: Labiola in Italy and Lagardelle in France frequently appeal from *Marx wrongly understood to Marx rightly understood*' (emphasis added).

When these critics quote Lenin to condemn and denounce the Party's tactics of united fronts with the democratic parties and groups, we cannot but conclude that they are exactly appealing from Lenin wrongly understood to Lenin rightly understood. How else can one understand them?

First of all, they, when quoting this passage of Lenin, do not care to understand either as to what the context was or what it was actually aiming at.

Lenin, in this famous article of his, was tracing how revisionist trends in the domain of philosophy, in the field of political economy, on the theory of crises, in the domain of politics, etc., had been developing for long in the working class movement of the west and how all of them 'constituted a fairly harmonious system of views, namely the old and well-known liberal system of views'.

He was castigating those socialist trends and leaders who had accepted the above-mentioned liberal bourgeois views, and who were going in for political 'agreements, alliances and blocs' with sections of the imperialist bourgeoisie. Do these comrades hold the view that our Party and its Central Committee are upholding such liberal bourgeois views on these and similar issues? Or that they are advocating fronts with imperialist bourgeoisie? If so, they have to substantiate it with facts. Otherwise it would be a gross slander on the Party's political line and the C.C. which is pursuing it.

Secondly, these comrades totally fail to understand the salient point, namely, Lenin's insistence that the revolutionary social-democratic parties of his day in the imperialist countries and states should not form 'alliances or blocs' with the liberal bourgeoisie of those countries and states, because they were bound to be counter-revolutionary. His specific mention of 'the social reform liberals in the west and liberal reformists (cadets) in the Russian revolution' does not permit of any confusion. Again the critics tend to ignore the fact that Lenin drew a clear distinction between the revolution in an imperialist country and the one in an oppressed country and permitted temporary agreements and alliances on certain conditions with the bourgeoisie of the oppressed countries by the proletariat and its Party.

Are not our critics here dogmatically attempting to apply Lenin's tactical directives to Communists of imperialist countries to those of backward and oppressed countries? Are they not also guilty of mechanically equating the democratic parties and groups which are in the united fronts of Kerala and West Bengal with the liberal bourgeoisie and its parties in the imperialist countries? Is it not precisely to defeat this type of left phrase-mongering that Stalin and the C.I. had to wage a bitter struggle? Let our comrades seriously ponder over it, before seeking support in Lenin's teachings for their fight against the Party's tactics of united fronts in Bengal and Kerala.

Thirdly, are these comrades doing justice to Lenin and his teachings on the united front tactics by invoking this specific quotation from him to fight against the united front tactics of our Party in Kerala and West Bengal?

Lenin also says: 'The more powerful enemy can be vanquished only by exerting the utmost effort, and by the most thorough, careful, attentive, skilful and *obligatory* use of any, even the smallest, rift between the enemies, any conflict of interests among the bourgeoisie of the various countries and among the various groups or types of bourgeoisie within the various countries, and also by taking advantage of any, even the smallest, opportunity of winning a mass ally, even though this ally is temporary, vacillating, unstable, unreliable and conditional. Those who do not understand this reveal a failure to understand even the smallest grain of Marxism, of modern scientific socialism *in general*. Those who have not proved *in practice*, over a fairly considerable period of time and in fairly varied political situations, their ability to apply this truth in practice have not yet learned to help the revolutionary class in its struggle to emancipate all toiling humanity from the exploiters. And this applies equally to the period *before* and after the proletariat has won political power.'

Do our comrades discover a howling contradiction between the two passages from Lenin, i.e., the one from his article on Marxism and Revisionism and the other from his book on 'Left'-Wing Communism? Is it not ridiculous in the extreme to quote the particular passage of Lenin and seek support in it for their repudiation of Communist united front tactics?

Lastly, our critics deliberately ignore the fact that our Party, consistent with the Marxist-Leninist dictums on the issue of united front tactics, scrupulously maintains its independent position, with its independent identity, organisation and programme, that it does not even permit the formation of blocs either inside or outside the legislatures; that it jealously reserves its right of independent action, both inside and outside the legislatures, notwithstanding the commonly agreed electoral and governmental minimum programme; and that it does not hesitate to openly demarcate with the decisions of the U.F. cabinets, if they are found to be in conflict with the declared aims and objectives of these fronts and governments. Are these such small details that our comrades can afford to bypass them and dub our tactics as on par with the revisionist tactics of Millerandism?

Let comrades pronounce as to whether there is anything common between the tactics advocated by these comrades regarding the Marxist-Leninist attitude to allies, and those advocated by Lenin. May we be enlightened by these comrades as to which are the parties and groups which are worthy of our alliance, if those in Kerala and West Bengal, today, are to be denounced as 'known reactionary forces'? Or is it their contention that every political party in the country, from the Congress to non-Congress democratic parties are reactionary, and hence our Party will have to go alone in fighting the reactionary Congress party and its government?

Contributors

PRASENJIT BOSE is Convenor of the Research Unit of the Communist Party of India (Marxist).

P.M.S. GREWAL is Secretary of the Delhi State Committee, and member of the Central Committee of the Communist Party of India (Marxist).

NILOTPAL BASU is member of the Central Secretariat of the Communist Party of India (Marxist).

VIJAY PRASHAD is George and Martha Kellner Chair in South Asian History and Professor of International Studies at Trinity College in Hartford, Connecticut, USA. He is the author of eleven books, including four for LeftWord Books.

Printed in Great Britain
by Amazon

79048800R00071